A *Life* of Broken Pieces Put Together by GOD

Steven Penrod

ISBN 979-8-89243-847-6 (paperback)
ISBN 979-8-89243-848-3 (digital)

Christian Faith Publishing
832 Park Avenue
Meadville, PA 16335
www.christianfaithpublishing.com

Printed in the United States of America

I wrote this book in memory of my wife, Leona. We had thirty-two beautiful years together. She wanted me to finish this book so much. But God took her to heaven on December 16, 2022. I just want to thank her for having so much faith and respect for me.

Chapter 1

My story began on May 21, 1953, at 9:55 a.m. My name is Steven Wayne Penrod. My mother's name is Geraldine R. Penrod; she was eighteen years old at the time of my birth. Her mother's name is Maxine A. Miller Penrod; her father's name is Virgil E. Penrod. When I was born in 1953, I was born at home and not in a hospital. I was told by my grandmother that the doctor who delivered me told my mother and grandmother to place hot bricks around me to keep me warm since I was not able to be placed in an incubator because I was born at home.

Because of the fact that I was not placed in an incubator, I had a lack of oxygen in my brain, and I do not know if there were other circumstances that caused me to be born with a disability. The disability I was born with was cerebral palsy. Because of my disability, I was unable to walk, and when I was two years old, I had surgery on my left eye for what they call lazy eye. I was told by my grandmother that when I was two years old, I was seen by my father, who never claimed me as his son, but that was the only time he ever saw me. But as you will see throughout the rest of my story, I believe that even then, God had other plans because, over the years, God has brought people into my life just the way God blessed me with a mother and grandmother who loved me in spite of my physical disability.

My guess is that my disability made it very difficult because they had to carry me around. When they did not carry me, I had to pull myself around using my arms or trying to crawl on my knees. So as you can see, it must have been very difficult for them, but I am very thankful that they were willing to make those daily sacrifices.

I have often wondered what would have happened if the doctor had known before I was born that I would have a disability; would he have told my mother to have an abortion as they sometimes do today? I am thankful that they were not aware of my disability because I often think of the many things I would have never experienced in my life. Because I know that God knew the things that I would face throughout my life, but I also know that God knew what was ahead of me even though I did not. I remember many times when my mother would go to work and did not have anyone to take care of me, so she would carry me to work with her, and she would find a place at work where I could go to sleep.

Eventually, my grandmother Maxine quit her job in Delaware, where she worked in a supermarket, to come back to Chillicothe, Ohio, to help take care of me. I don't remember exactly when, but there came a point in time when I had an operation to try to spread my legs apart to help me learn to walk.

When I had the surgery, each leg was put in a plaster cast with a plaster bar in between them while I recovered from the surgery. That surgery took place at Children's Hospital in Columbus, Ohio, which is now known as Nationwide Children's Hospital. The doctor who performed most, but not all, of my surgery was an orthopedic surgeon who also traveled to other countries around the world to teach other doctors how to perform different types of orthopedic surgery; his name was Dr. Worstell.

As I remember, there was an apartment that was upstairs on the corner of Main Street and Cutright Drive, and it is still there today, but I remember one time, and I don't know if we were living there or went to visit someone else who lived there, but I was still in the cast with the bar in between, recovering from my first surgery, and the apartment was upstairs, so it took at least two people to carry me up the stairs with the casts on my legs.

I can still remember having to go to physical therapy, and at that time, Mount Logan School had a therapy room within the school building. I can also remember having to ride a city bus from wherever we were living at that time to go to physical therapy at Mount Logan.

On November 21, 1959, my mother married Forest E. Blazer Jr. I am very thankful to him for raising me to become the man I am today. I can never repay him for raising me and teaching me not to give up and not to stop trying. There was a saying that he taught me when I was small; it was that "can't" crawled under a log and died, and "try" took its place. It was true then, and it is still true today. Most of the surgery on my legs took place after I started school when I was in the first or second grade. It seems like they always scheduled my surgeries before the end of the school year so that I would have the summer to recover. I remember one year in particular, it must have been either 1960 or 1961, when I was chosen to be the poster child for the Ross County Easter Seal Society, and it just so happened that I was in Children's Hospital in Columbus, recovering from one of my many surgeries, and it just so happened to be over Easter that year. I have a picture of me sitting in my hospital bed, surrounded by four or five Easter baskets, and there is a nurse in the picture with me, and the caption of the picture states that I was the Easter Seal poster child for Ross County. As I said, this was one of the many times in my early years that God was watching over me. There were a couple of things that, in many ways, were very funny and, at the same time, very thoughtful. One was that it seemed like everyone who came into my room at the hospital would end up signing the casts that were on my legs after surgery. The other was the fact that if I could get them to give me a wheelchair so I could get around in it, I used to try to chase and run over all the nurses in the hallway of the hospital. I would usually have to wear the casts for four to six weeks following each surgery. When I was little, I did not realize how they removed each cast. I used to think that they used a regular saw to cut the casts off of my legs, but I later realized that they used a vibrating saw that would cause the casts to crack so they could remove them from my legs, and then they would take out my stitches, which sometimes did not feel very good.

And then when I went home, I would always take the casts with me, and my mother kept each one of them. When I first learned to walk, I had to use wooden crutches that went up underneath each arm, and for several years, I had to wear braces on each leg.

I remember each time I would need special shoes, crutches, and braces, it would mean another trip to Columbus. There was a place in Columbus, Ohio, I think it was a medical supply store, so I could get the special shoes, crutches, and braces that I had to have.

My dad and I were talking one night on the phone, and he told me that the reason he did not adopt me when he and my mother got married in 1959 was that he knew he could not afford to pay for my surgeries or other medical needs.

I have two other sisters and another brother. My brother's name is Eddie Blazer; my sisters' names are Tracey D. Blazer and Teresa. My brother, Eddie, and my sister Teresa are from his previous marriage before he married my mother.

When I started school at Mount Logan, we lived in an apartment building on Fourth Street. I remember living upstairs, so when I would go up and down the stairs, I would have to sit down and slide down the stairs and move my crutches, sliding them down the stairs as well. When I would go upstairs, it was almost the same process, except I had to crawl on my hands and knees until I got to the top of the stairs, and then I would have to take one crutch and hold on to the railing to stand up. When I started school, there was a handicap class at Mount Logan School for other handicapped students like myself.

The teacher of the handicapped class was a lady; her name was Mrs. Lucille Carter. As I mentioned earlier, there is also a picture of me sitting at my desk in school with Mrs. Carter standing beside my desk. The picture was taken the year that I was chosen as the Easter Seal poster child for the Ross County chapter. Some of the other students in the handicap class with me were Rosalie Parks, Terry Gallagher, and Susie Alexander; her father, Clark Alexander, was a former mayor of Chillicothe, Ohio. Also, one of my former classmates was Theodore Fickisen, who was a very good artist when we were in school, and he later became the curator of the Pump House art gallery in Yoctangee Park in Chillicothe, Ohio. There were many other students in the handicap class with us.

I remember when I was younger, my father worked at Brewer and Brewer gravel plant on, wait a minute, Three Locks Road. He used to run heavy equipment there. I still remember that he had to pay fifteen dollars a week in child support for my brother Eddie and my sister Terry; he made approximately ninety dollars, so we lived on seventy-five dollars a week. For me, things were different back then than they are today. I did not realize that we were poor because it seemed that we had what we needed. I remember in the early 1960s, we moved to a farm on Baptist Hill Road.

Chapter 2

When we moved to the farm, I was still using wooden crutches. I can remember in the wintertime when we used to have a lot of snow, and I would be outside trying to walk with my crutches. Sometimes the snow would be up to my knees, but I was still able to get around in the deep snow we used to have in the wintertime many years ago.

I also used to have a dog; his name was Sport, and one day he came up missing, and I never really knew what happened to him. We had a neighbor, and I do not think he liked Sport very much. When we moved to the farm, I then had to board out in town all week to go to school at Mount Logan. When I had to board out while going to school, I would either go to the house at which I was staying on Sunday night or early Monday morning. There were other classmates who had to do the same thing.

I stayed in several different homes over the years. I had a classmate named Freddy; his home was the first home in which I stayed while going to school. Another place I stayed while going to school was not too far from Freddy's house.

The lady who lived in that house was an older lady; her name was Vadia Lot. She had an older son; his name was Richard, who also lived with her. I lived with them for a couple of years. One of the other things that I remember while living with her were the times during the spring and in the fall when you could hear the bell letting you know the ice cream man was coming down the street, so all of the kids would run outside to get ice cream from him, especially me.

One of my fondest memories was something that happened one Friday night while I was waiting for my ride to go home for the weekend because we were still living on the farm. One Friday night, my grandmother Maxine stopped at the house where I was staying and gave me a black cocker spaniel that she bought from a man who was moving to a place where he could not keep the dog. She gave the man fifty dollars for the dog and brought the dog to me as I was waiting for my ride to go home for the weekend. Richard tried to take my dog, and I got mad at him and told him he could not have my dog. She was totally black, except for one white spot in the shape of a diamond on her neck. So because of that, I named her Cinder.

When we lived on the farm, our house was at the end of the lane. We had next-door neighbors; their names were Jim and Jeanette Oats. They had two children, Jimmy and Jerry. Jerry was a girl, and sometimes the three of us would play with each other, but most of the time, I played by myself. There was one time when Jimmy was outside in the yard, and there happened to be a skunk walking around the yard with a can on its head. Jimmy walked right up to the skunk and took the can off the skunk's head, and it did not offer to spray him. Someone happened to take a picture when that happened.

I had a sand pile outside that I used to play in with my Tonka toys when I played by myself. But since we lived on a farm that had a lot of trees, I used to go back into the woods with a hatchet and chop down trees just to have something to do and to be outside. Wherever I went, my dog Cinder was always with me. We had a cow, so when I would go back in the woods, I would have to crawl under the barbed wire fence. When Cinder knew I was going outside, she would follow me everywhere I went. Whenever I had to crawl under the fence, she had the habit of going under the fence, and then I would get down on my hands and knees and push my crutches under the fence, and then I would crawl under the fence myself. Then I would stand up, and once she knew I was standing up, she would walk a certain distance ahead of me, then she would sit down and wait until I got up to where she was, and she would go on a little farther and do the same thing. And whenever I would get to wherever I was going in the woods, she would always stay very close to me. I always had the feeling that she knew she was supposed to watch out for me, and she did.

One time, when my mother went to town, she let me stay home because I was playing with the neighbors' kids, Jimmy and Jerry Oates. We were playing hide and seek. I was trying to hide from Jimmy and Jerry when I stepped down into a low place where I thought I could hide from them, but I accidentally fell and hit my head on a drain tile, and I think I passed out because the next thing I remember was Jeanette carrying me across the yard to her house because my head was bleeding. But she was able to stop the bleeding by the time my mother got home.

While living on the farm, we grew our own food, did our own canning, raised our own animals, and did our own butchering. We went to my granddad Blazer's farm because he had a smokehouse for when we did the pork to hang them for smoking. He had an old iron kettle, and we would make our own lard and homemade crackling. Everything we ate, we knew what it was because we raised all of it. I had to help my mother do the canning. We'd have green beans, corn, and many other things. We had a blackberry patch and cherry trees in the field and would pick the berries. Mom would make jelly from them. We didn't have to worry about the food making us sick. We rarely had to buy our own food. We did our own remodeling. I'd put black adhesive, like tar, on the wall, and I had to hold it up until it would stick to the wall. But as you see, I still had to help out on the farm even with my handicap.

We also had to cut our own firewood, and my dad would cut trees with a chainsaw. We had an old saw like at a sawmill but could run it with a tractor with a belt. When the wood was cut, I'd have to load it on the wagon. Then we would take the tractor with the wood to the house. We had a metal door that was like a coal bin to deposit it into the furnace. He'd take the tractor, and we'd drive to the house and park it. We would take a chisel and split the bigger pieces in two. I'd have to take the smaller logs and throw them into the coal bin in the house.

As you can see, I really had no limitations because I learned to do everything I had to do on the farm. We were still living on the farm in 1963. On Friday, November 22, we were sitting in class when Mrs. Carter came back from the office and turned on the TV in the room. That was when all the kids realized President Kennedy had been shot. When I got home that night, my mom and dad had bought our first colored TV. All that weekend and through all of the things with the president's funeral, my mother was trying to take pictures off of the TV with the camera, which did not work. But I remember, even though I wasn't very old, that's when things started to change. But there were a lot of good memories when living on the farm because I had responsibilities.

One time, my dad went to the stock sale and bought a calf. I was sick in bed with mumps and chicken pox. It was so cold he could not leave the calf outside, so he carried it through the house to the basement and built a pen for it to stay in until the weather warmed up. He told me it was my responsibility to take care of it.

In 1965, we moved to Rozelle Creek. I was about thirteen when I met Carol Sue Sutherland Witcom. I gave her the nickname Red due to her bright-red hair. She is still one of my best friends to this day. I was the type that always wanted to be outside. Carol had a sister named Cathy who was the exact opposite because she always wanted to be with their mother. But Carol was always with me, doing the same things I was. We had a great big field between our houses and the neighbors. Carol and I would go out and dig holes. We used to say we were digging into China. When the hole got really deep, Carol said she was going to leave me at the bottom. I would complain, saying, "No, you can't leave me here. You have to help me out of the hole!"

During the week, I would go to Mount Logan School and, on weekends, stay at my friend's house, playing games. We used to have ice cube fights. I couldn't run, so they would hit me in the neck all the time. Our home had a garage on one end and a breezeway on the other. Dad decided he wanted to move the garage to the other side of the house in order to install indoor plumbing. Before that, we had an outhouse, and one thing I always hated about it was how cold it got inside.

When I was sick, I had to be carried to the outhouse, so having indoor plumbing made things easier. I often helped my mother with her renovation projects. I remember when she wanted to tear out the breezeway. I would be on my hands and knees with a hammer and mixing paddle, putting up drywall with her. Another time, Mother decided she wanted a half basement. Part of the house had a cistern for water, so there was not enough room to do a full basement. So I told her that if she would move the wheel barrel, I would dig out under the basement. I loved to dig in the dirt.

So when I'd fill the wheel barrel, she would dump it. I'd do as much as I could but eventually needed help to do the rest, so I talked my neighbor into helping me. He had trouble doing his spelling, and since that was my best subject in school, I made him a deal. If he helped with the basement, I would help with his spelling. Finally, the half-basement was finished.

During one of my birthdays, my grandfather Virgil Pennrod would stop by and give me a dollar. The dollar from him was more important to me than anything else. I knew that he did not have a lot of money, and his thoughtfulness meant a lot. During one of my summers, I lived in Knockemstiff with my grandfather, and I grew up with his kids. Granddad's kids were Treva; Sandy; Linda; Billy; Corey; Eddy, one who had passed; Mike; and Cherry. We all grew up together, and I'd go and spend time with them at Knockemstiff. We'd pick up pop bottles and turn them in for money. Granddad would also give us a dollar. After collecting, we would go to the store and buy penny candy.

My uncle Earnest was married to Pricilla Penrod. I found out years later that her son Max was in the navy. Max would visit his mother when he was on furlough. When I started going to church on Watt Street, his wife, Charlotte, was going to church at the time. She would go home and tell him about me. It jogged his memory about the times I'd visit his mother. We would have the Penrod reunion in Yoctangee Park around the Fourth of July. Our reunions often consisted of one hundred people or more. Some of my relatives included Aunt Esta Hawk Penrod; Aunt Tiny; Uncle Budd, who used to sell bottled gas for the stove; Uncle Fred, who was married to Dorothy; Uncle Dene, who used to work on TV sets; Shep Penrod; and Jane Long Penrod, who was related to the people who run Wares Funeral Home.

Many of my family members played instruments, but by the time they finished playing their music, they would usually be drunk.

There were a lot of wonderful memories in Knockemstiff. When we would have our reunion, there was usually a carnival in the park. The kids would go to the carnival and spend time there and go back and forth. All the carnies would let me get on for as long as I wanted. I used to play games while I was there. One game had slots with numbers on it. You would roll a ball down it and would get points for prizes. The carny who ran it would let me cheat; he thought that if other kids watched me play, they may try to give it a go as well, seeing how their luck would fare.

By the time I returned to the reunion, I would have a bunch of toys. One of the games was a ring toss. You would win the bottle of pop it landed on. I would trade them for other toys with the kids. I did a lot of different things in my life that a lot of people would not try. I used to go to summer camp at Camp Pitchinger; it was almost to the border of Ohio. When we would go to camp, Hibiys's funeral home would take us there and put our luggage in the hearse. It is now known as Howlers' Funeral Home today, the very one my pastor works for. One time, I remember asking the driver of the hearse, "Can you hear the embalming fluid when moving a body?" He said that he could.

I asked another question, "What would you do if the person sat up and said something?"

He said he would leave the hearse and take off running.

I would go to camp with a lot of kids from school; it was for handicapped kids. We would stay for two weeks. We would clean our cabins every day, and the kid with the cleanest cabin would win candy. It was for both boys and girls, with the boys' camp being in the very back. We would have to walk back and forth to get to the activities. Every morning, they would blow a trumpet like in the military and raise the flag. A lot of things that happened at camp showed how God would take care of me. A couple of times at the camp, I could have been hurt or killed, but God was taking care of me despite myself.

One time, we had a dance and a swimming pool, and I didn't have trunks and wanted to get in the pool. The camp counselor let me swim in my clothing. I couldn't swim but would float in the pool on an inner tube. I fell into the water and started to drown. A counselor saved me. Along the edge of the camp was a ravine with a bridge across it. If you were not careful, you could fall in. When we were being brave, we would make the bridge swing. Due to the boys' camp being in the very back, I would get tired, so the kids would offer to put me in a wagon.

One time, we raced the wagon, and it fell into the ravine. I fell with it and landed on a drainpipe. Thank God I was not hurt. It happened a second time, and that prompted the counselors to put up a fence. Despite all these accidents, I never once broke a bone. During an overnight camp out in the woods, they premade hamburgers, onions, and potatoes wrapped in foil. We'd put the food in the fire to cook it. There was a kid during the campout giving me a hard time. He said he could beat the crap out of me, so I told him, "Let's settle it."

The counselors let the two of us fight; both they and the kids were placing bets. We started to wrestle, and after a while, I got him down and started beating on him a little. I tried to get him to say "uncle" several times; finally, he gave up. I learned that if anyone tried to tell me I could not do something, I would stubbornly try to do it anyway just to prove them wrong. That's how I learned to defend myself.

After returning from camp, a few months later, on December 25, 1971, my parents got a phone call that night. They said that Granddad was not doing well. My parents took off to Knockemstiff, and Mom told me that Cathy and Sue could stay with me. We had a pool table in the living room. I had to call my grandmother about Granddad not being in good shape. While the girls were playing, I would walk around the pool table. Carol said I was cheating. So I said, "It's in my house, and it's my pool table." She came up behind me, and we tripped and fell. I asked her if she was trying to break my leg. She said not particularly, but that I was still cheating. Later that night, my grandfather passed away. It's one of the reasons I don't like to celebrate Christmas too much.

Chapter 3

In the fall of 1971, I discussed with the Ohio Department of Rehabilitation the possibility of getting some job training, given that I was not returning to school at Mount Logan. After some discussion, my case manager from the Ohio Department of Rehabilitation told me I could go to Cincinnati to the Goodwill Rehabilitation and Training Center.

The Goodwill Rehabilitation and Training Center, located on Springfield Pike in Woodlawn, Ohio, a suburb of Cincinnati, would test each client to see what abilities they had for different jobs. They tested me at many jobs, such as working in an office answering phones and taking messages, working in a mailroom as if I were in a post office sorting mail, and as a possible bookkeeper by having me balance charts and graphs like you would have to do when bookkeeping for a business. Once the testing was done, they realized that none of the testing was or anything that I would have an easy time doing because working in an office, I could not take dictation, type fast, or write fast enough to take messages. Working in a mailroom in a post office was not possible because I could not stand for long periods, and I was not interested in bookkeeping, even though I was very good with numbers.

However, there was a sheltered workshop at Goodwill where they did chair caning, so they decided to let me try that. Once I did, they realized that chair caning was a good fit for me for two reasons: one, I could sit while doing the chair caning; and two, I was good with my hands, and a lot of the chair caning had to be done by hand. Thus, the tools I needed were paid for and provided by the Ohio Department of Rehabilitation Services.

When I went to Cincinnati for training, that was the first time I had ever been away from home, other than the two weeks every summer I had spent at Camp Pittenger. It was the first time I had been on my own for an extended period. The Goodwill Training Center had dormitories on the premises for clients not from Cincinnati. That was the first time I had to learn how to do my own laundry; they also had washers and dryers for the clients to wash their clothes. I also had to do my own ironing. As you can see, that was a very important time in my life when I was learning not only what it was to work at a job but also how to do other daily life tasks.

When I went to work in the chair caning shop, I made a lot of new friends. I also learned that this was the only department in Goodwill where people who had cane furniture could bring it to have it repaired; it was the only department that did restoration work for the general public. When a person would bring in their furniture to be repaired, if they wished to have their furniture refinished before it was repaired, they would be quoted a price, which included refinishing the furniture plus repairing the back or bottom of the furniture.

If the furniture needed to be refinished, it was taken downstairs to the basement, where the old finish was stripped off and sanded down, and a new stain was applied. Once that was done, the furniture was returned to our department, where we would make the necessary repairs. A lot of the caning that was done had to be done by hand, but there were other types of repairs that we also did. Some chairs had what is called a rush bottom, other chairs were repaired with what we called pressed cane, and we would also repair wicker furniture. As you can see, there were many different kinds of things going on within our shop.

All of the people who worked in our shop were, in one way or another, disabled. There were two men in our shop who were blind. One young man in our shop, named Mike, was blind, and the other gentleman, Mr. Edward Smith, who was in his seventies, was also blind. Not only was he blind, but he also had an artificial limb; one of his legs had been amputated, and he had an artificial leg. There were several things about Mr. Smith that amazed me: one was that he had to do his chair caning mostly by feel, and usually when he was working on a chair, he would take off his artificial leg and set it beside the chair on which he was sitting. The most amazing thing about him was that every day when we would go to lunch, he would take the money out of his wallet before we headed for the cafeteria, and sometimes by the feel of the money or by sticking it under the bright light by his workbench, he could tell the denomination of the bill that he would use to pay for his lunch.

The boss of our shop was a man who had clubbed feet; he walked on the sides of his ankles. His name was David Shaw, and he was a very nice man who would later on become a very good friend of mine, as you will find out through the rest of this chapter. When we would go to lunch, David Shaw and I would lead Mr. Smith and Mike to the cafeteria for lunch. Most of the time, it was just the four of us in the shop, but once in a while, there would be other people in the shop for possible training. We had a lot of good times while working in the shop because back in the seventies, the Cincinnati Reds had a lot of day games that were on the radio. At that time, we had a radio in our shop, so we would listen to the Reds games while we were working. That was back in the beginning years of the Big Red Machine, and since I was living in Cincinnati at that time, I was able to attend many Reds baseball games.

Since I was in training, we had a 10:30 p.m. curfew. If any of us were going to be out late, we had to get permission to stay out past curfew. But if we were going to the Reds game, there was a gentleman who worked at Goodwill who would drive us to the ballpark and drop us off. Then it was our responsibility to find a way home after the game. One day, there were three of us who went to the Reds game. The gentleman dropped us off as he usually did, so we watched the game that night. As we were leaving Riverfront Stadium, we had to find a taxi. The three of us counted our money to see how much we had between us, and we had twenty-seven dollars. When we found a taxi, we told him where we needed to go, but we also told him that we only had twenty-seven dollars between us. We told him we needed to go to Goodwill in Woodlawn. He told us to get in. The taxi even turned on the meter and drove until the meter hit twenty-seven dollars. He then turned off the meter and took us the rest of the way to Goodwill without the meter running.

I was still seventeen years old when I first went to Cincinnati, but shortly thereafter, I turned eighteen and met my first girlfriend. At first, I thought she was a very nice girl, and as a young teenager, of course, I thought I was in love. There came a short time later when I thought we were going to get married, so I rode the bus back to Chillicothe to get my birth certificate. When my grandmother picked me up at the bus station, I told her to go to my mother's house because I wanted my mother to go get my birth certificate. I told her if she did not go get it, I would go get it. So my grandmother, who happened to be living in an upstairs apartment on Main Street, got to the point that I had even purchased an engagement ring for the girl I thought I was going to marry. My mother did go and get my birth certificate as I had asked her to do. But when she brought it to my grandmother's apartment, she started to tell me that I should not get married, at which point I told her I was eighteen years old and not to tell me what to do because it was my decision. If it was a mistake, it would be on me and not on her. I also told her that I did not want to be angry with her for telling me what to do.

But as it turned out, God had another plan for my life because the two of us did not get married after all. Once I finished my training, I decided to return to Chillicothe and start a chair caning business there. Of course, that did not work out because there was no call for chair caning in Chillicothe. So I did some checking and found out I would be able to return to Goodwill and go back to work in the chair caning department there, which I did.

Right before I had gone to Cincinnati the first time, I had begun receiving Supplemental Security Income, which had previously been Aid for the Disabled, which I had received previously through the Ross County Welfare Department. When I started working at Goodwill in the caning department, I was making $4.15 an hour. So at that point, I was still staying in the dormitory at Goodwill. It was about that time that I met a gentleman named Harry McNaughton. It also happened that Harry was from Chillicothe. He told me later that his grandmother had owned the Lincoln Inn and the Old Virginia Home, which happened to be two bars located right next to each other on US 23 South between Chillicothe and Waverly. Harry and I became very close friends and, in some ways, watched out for each other. He would watch out for me so that other people did not try to hurt or take advantage of me, and I would watch out for him because I knew he had epileptic seizures and sometimes did not take his medication. Of course, I would try to make sure he took it as prescribed. He was a cook in the cafeteria at Goodwill. Harry usually worked weekends and did most of the cooking. Since I did not go to Chillicothe very often, there came a point when I bought a portable radio. On the weekends when Harry worked, I would get up at 5:00 a.m., get dressed, take my radio to the cafeteria, and Harry and I would sit and drink coffee, smoke cigarettes, and listen to country music all day long.

When I first got to Goodwill, they had a cigarette machine in the hallway. When the cigarettes went to two dollars a pack, I decided to quit smoking because I did not have a lot of money. But one of the things I still remember to this day, as if it happened yesterday, was the first time I saw one of my roommates trying to sniff airplane glue to get high. That was about the time that people were trying to find different ways to get high, whether it was smoking marijuana or sniffing glue that was used to put models together. I remember many times when I would go into the restroom, and you could tell that someone had been smoking marijuana in the restroom.

There were times when the food in the cafeteria was not very good, or they were having something that some of us did not like. There were two places close by where you could go get something else to eat. One was a steakhouse at the top of the hill close to Goodwill itself. I ate at that steakhouse many times. There was also an establishment across the road from Goodwill on Springfield Pike called the Century Inn. It was originally a stagecoach stop from back in the 1800s. It was a restaurant and a bar, so you could either get something to eat or you could go get an alcoholic beverage, whichever you chose. There was one night when several of us from Goodwill decided to go over to the Century Inn. When we got there, we decided to order a pitcher of beer because back then, you could buy a pitcher of beer for a dollar. But one of the gentlemen that went with us was Mike, my coworker from the chair caning shop, and as I mentioned previously, he was blind. So when the waitress came to our table to take our order, she carded Mike to check his age. He was very upset by the fact that I was younger than he was, and she had carded him but did not card me. When we went to work the next morning, he was still fuming over it.

There was another time when several of us decided to go back to the Century Inn. But when you cross Springfield Pike, you would go about halfway across and have to stop because there was traffic coming the other way. The people I was with had all crossed the road ahead of me. I was about halfway across and looked both ways, and there was nothing coming. But the next thing I heard was brakes squealing, and as I turned to look, there was a car that hadn't stopped, and there was less than a foot between me and the front of the car. But I felt as though God had put himself or an angel between me and the front of that car because, by all rights, the car should have hit me. The only thing I could do was turn around, look at the lady, tell her I was sorry, and walk across the street. So that was another time, even in spite of what I was doing and in spite of the fact that God knew where I was going, he was watching out for me, even though I ended up doing something that I am not proud of. But if I want my book to tell my story the way it happened, both the good and the bad, to let anyone who reads this book know that God is always there to watch out for us, even if we are in the process of doing something that he wishes we would not do, and the fact that he loves us in spite of our faults and failures.

As our group entered the Century Inn that Friday night, there was no place to sit. There was a great big table in the middle of the room, but when we walked in, Mr. Floor, the head of Goodwill, and the training director, who happened to be my boss, were sitting at the big table with some other people. So we had to wait until the people at the big table left before we could even sit down. Then we all started drinking, and I made one mistake in the fact that I had not eaten anything earlier that day. So several hours later, I decided to get something to eat and then I had to go to the restroom. And when I came back, I suppose whoever I was with realized that I was drunk enough that I would do anything, so they dared me to make a pass at a woman in the bar, which I did. But luckily, I think she knew I was drunk and did not respond. But later, when I thought we were all leaving, we headed toward the door, and once we got outside and the air hit me, I realized that I was so drunk that I could not stand up, even on my crutches. So two of the guys I was with picked me up, one on each side, and carried me across the highway and put me down in the parking lot of Goodwill. Then as we walked back toward the dormitory and got up the ramp and inside the building, once again, I had to go to the restroom. So they waited until I came out, then they had to try to sneak me back to the room without Mrs. Leach seeing me and finding out how drunk I was because if I had gotten caught, I could have been kicked out of the program at Goodwill. So they got me back to the room and put me in bed, and then they decided they were going back over to the bar. So I dozed off, but when I woke up, I needed to go to the restroom, and I thought to myself, *If I can get to the door and slide down the wall to the bathroom without getting caught, I would be fine because the restroom was in the hallway.* So I got out of bed and started toward the door, but somehow I did not reach the door because I ended up sliding down the wall and sitting on the floor underneath the sink in our room. Then all at once, I realized I was about to throw up, so I grabbed a hold of the sink to try to stand up and ended up throwing up in the sink. Once I threw up, I decided just to go back to bed. So on my hands and knees, I crawled across the floor, pushing my crutches as I went, and then I was able to get back in bed and went to sleep.

The next morning, my roommate and I had kind of slept in, so when we got up, my roommate went to try to find a janitor so he could get something to clean out the sink trap where I had gotten sick the night before. Then it was around lunchtime, so both of us headed for the cafeteria, and it just so happened that Ms. Leach was sitting at one of the tables in the cafeteria when we walked in. There happened to be a gentleman there who took pictures for Goodwill Industries, and that was about the time that my mustache started coming in. So the photographer decided he was going to take a black pencil and try to darken my mustache. As we ate lunch, I wondered if Mrs. Leach had known that I had gotten drunk the night before. If she did, nothing was ever said about it, and I am very thankful for that because, even in spite of me doing that, I know God was not pleased with it; He took care of me in spite of myself. And it just so happened that later that day, all of the people at Goodwill were going bowling. Now I had bowled before, but I had never bowled a very high score. But the strange thing was, that Saturday, I bowled the highest score I had ever bowled in my life: the score was 113.

As I spent most of the early '70s living in Cincinnati, I became a very big Reds fan. I was lucky enough to find a speaker that would plug into the headphone jack of my radio so that if the Reds were playing out on the West Coast and the game did not start until nine or ten at night, I could still listen to the game and not disturb my roommates because that speaker went under my pillow.

There came a time when I was able to rent a house down the street from Goodwill. The Goodwill bus would pick me up for work around 7:30 a.m., and then they would have to make their rounds to pick up other employees. We would get back to Goodwill about 8:30 a.m., which was a half-hour before we started working at 9:00 a.m. There was a nurse who worked at Goodwill; her name was Mark Schultz. She had been born with polio, and she rode around on a three-wheel scooter. At one point in time, I had to take medicine every day because I carried the TB germ, but I was not allowed to take the medicine at home. I had to take it at work, so that meant every day, I would have to go to her office to get my medication from her. She was a very nice lady, but sometimes I would get very upset with her because one time she told me I was fat and needed to go on a diet. So she put me on a diet and told the dietitian that the only thing I could eat was what they were told her to fix for me to eat, which included salad and several other things I didn't like very well. That went on for a while, but one day, while I was walking back from the front of Goodwill in Dexter, where the Goodwill store was located, I happened to run into her, and she told me that I looked like I had lost some weight and to keep up whatever I was doing. But little did she know that I was eating whatever I wanted, including ice cream. One of my favorite flavors of ice cream is White House ice cream, which is vanilla ice cream with maraschino cherries in it. One of my other favorite flavors of ice cream is mint chocolate chip.

There finally came a time when they decided to close the chair caning shop at Goodwill and, as I believe I stated earlier, the services that they provided to the general public. While I was still living at Goodwill, I met my second girlfriend, and her name was Barbara. I don't know how she and I got hooked up with a couple of people that we met while we were trying to date. One of the people was a gentleman who was in training in the watch repair shop at Goodwill, who happened to be in a wheelchair and happened to be my roommate at one point. But one weekend came, and a lady that he wanted to date asked Barbara and me if we would go and stay at her house for the weekend, and we said yes, not knowing that she was planning on running off with the guy who worked in the watch shop. We did not find out what they were planning to do until after we had gotten to her house, and then she proceeded to tell us that if her husband asked where she was, we were to tell him we did not know where she was. Thankfully, we did not. Eventually, her husband came home and asked where she had gone, and we stated that we did not know, but we told him that we needed to return to Goodwill. So thankfully, he took us back to Goodwill, and no one ever discovered what was really going on because if they had, both of us could have been kicked out of the program. A couple of days later, my roommate returned and came into the room one night very upset because the lady he had wanted to run off with broke up with him. Because he was so distraught, he decided to put his fist through a plate glass window and said he wanted to kill himself. That happened to be the second time in my life when I was trying to keep someone from committing suicide. Luckily, we had a button by our beds in our dorm rooms that, in case of emergency, we could push. So I pushed the button, and Mrs. Leach asked me what was wrong. When I told her what was happening, she must have known that she needed to call the police because a little while later, at least two officers came to the room and took him away. He must have been kicked out of the program because I never saw him again.

It was about that time when I rented the house that I lived in once I moved out of the dormitory at Goodwill, but just prior to that, I was preparing to celebrate my birthday, and I wanted to have a cookout and cake for my birthday. So I asked the lady who ran the kitchen if she would allow me to order steaks and corn on the cob through Goodwill, which she did. But not only that, she also had the people who worked in the kitchen make baked beans and salad for my birthday, which was something that she did not have to do. There was one time when she was very angry because one Sunday morning, when Harry was working, he had me back in the kitchen with him while he was preparing something to be eaten later that day. Well, I was back there, she walked in, and she told Harry, "You know he's not supposed to be back here."

But Harry told her, "I know that, but I want him back here." So she never said anything, and nothing else was ever said about it. But that had happened before I asked her to order that stuff for my birthday party. That might have happened to be a lot of fun because I had friends around, and we cooked the steaks on a grill with my corn on the cob and the rest of the food for my birthday, including my birthday cake.

When they finally did close the chair painting department, they gave me all the customer lists and everything else involved with that, so I was practically handed my own business. So I ran the business out of my house. People would call and make an appointment to bring their chairs or other furniture to be repaired, but the nice thing about that was the fact that I could set my own hours and work as long as I wanted. And the house, which I was renting, provided the perfect setup for my situation because I can do the chair caning in my basement. I had an adjustable bench built for me where I could clamp the chairs on the bench and raise the bench up and down to the height I needed it to be. What I was doing, I also had a metal sink that stood on two legs where I could run buckets of hot water to soak the cane. There were some nights when I didn't have anything to watch on television or anything else to do, and if I had furniture that needed to be finished, I would go downstairs, sometimes at seven or seven thirty, and sometimes I may work until two or three in the morning because I had my radio to listen to, and there was nobody in the house but me.

There was one time when I got a phone call from someone asking if they could bring a chair by to see if I could fix it, so I told them yes, they could come by and let me look at it. When they got there, they were an older couple. The gentleman looked like he was about six feet, five inches tall. His wife was not as quite as tall as he was, but when I looked at the chair, the center of the seat had been torn out of it, and it was a chair that had holes that you had to cane by hand. So I proceeded to ask them how it had gotten broken out, and one of them said that their son had been standing on it, trying to do something else, and his foot went through the seat of the chair. As I looked at his parents, I thought to myself, *I wonder who their son is*, and then I was shocked because they proceeded to tell me that their son was Dave Cowens, the forward and/or center of the Boston Celtics. When I had finished repairing the chair and they came to pick it up, besides paying for having the chair fixed, they gave me a postcard with him in his Celtics uniform.

There was another time when I had a person call me and asked if they could come see me, and I said yes. The gentleman told me that he had found some old wood in a barn and wanted to build his wife a rocking chair out of it, and he wanted to know what he had to do. So when he arrived at my house, he brought the pieces of the chair with him, and when I saw the wood, I was totally amazed because the wood he had found was solid cherry, and he had already cut the pieces for the chair, and he wanted to know what he had to do because he wanted a hand cane bottom and back in the rocking chair. So I told him that he would have to go home and drill holes around the edge of the back and the bottom of the chair, and then bring it back to me, and I would put the back and the bottom in it. But I told him to count the holes around the back and the bottom because it cost about thirty cents a hole to do a hand cane chair. When he returned with the chair, he had put the chair together, but he had also put the stain on the chair, and I realized that when I finished it, it would end up being one of the pieces of furniture that I was most proud to have worked on. That happened to be one of those situations that I talked about earlier when I said that if I did not have anything to watch on TV, I would go downstairs and start working and sometimes work till almost daylight. I remember that it took me approximately three or four days to finish the chair, but when I called him and told him the chair was finished, and he came to pick it up, he told me that whatever it had cost him to build the chair and have me put that back and bottom in it was worth it because, as I remember, it was a gift for his wife.

There are a couple of other things that stand out in my memory of the time that I spent in Cincinnati. I met a young man who worked in the kitchen at Goodwill; his name was David Johnson, and he needed a place to stay. I happened to have a spare bedroom, so he rented that spare bedroom, and as I remember, I think I only charged him about fifty dollars a month. But back then, you could live a lot cheaper than you could today. There were times when he and I did several things together. If he didn't want to cook at the house, we did not live too far from a White Castle, so we would go to White Castle and order about thirty to forty hamburgers and two or three orders of french fries apiece, and then we would come home and sit in the living room floor, eat White Castles, and watch TV.

There had been another occasion while I was still living in the dormitory at Goodwill, but David and I had become friends, and one day, we decided we were going to the Reds game. I had just purchased a chevron popcorn popper, and while we were sitting in the rec room, I decided we were going to pop popcorn to take to the baseball game. But the only sack we had was a Goodwill bag that was over a foot long, so we popped two or three batches of popcorn, put it in the bag, and left for Riverfront Stadium. Now we did not know whether or not they would even let us take it into the ballpark, but luckily, the guy at the gate must have felt sorry for us because he told us we could take it into the ballpark. So the two of us sat there, eating our own popcorn and watching the baseball game, and as I remember, the only things we bought that day were something to drink and some ice cream because it was hot.

One of the other things that I remember, which makes me think back, is something I said earlier about Harry McNaughten, about him having epileptic seizures. There was one night when Harry got off work, and he asked a bunch of us boys if we would take him to his apartment, and of course, we said we would. When we got to his apartment, I realized it was up a long flight of stairs, and I thought to myself, *How am I going to get up all those stairs?* because they were very steep. But all at once, Harry picked me up, threw me over his shoulder, carried me up the stairs, and then I sat down in the chair in his living room. Then he asked us if we wanted a beer. Of course, we were stupid and said yes. But as we sat in his living room, his landlord showed up, and all at once, Harry began to have an epileptic seizure. I don't know whether the landlord did not know what to do or not, but he started to stick his fingers in Harry's mouth, and I spoke up and told him not to do that because Harry could have bitten his fingers off. So I told him to take a spoon and hold Harry's tongue down so that it did not roll up in his mouth. A little while later, after Harry had passed out, he finally came to, and the landlord told Harry he was calling the squad to take him to the hospital. Of course, Harry refused to go to the hospital, so I told the landlord we would take him back to Goodwill, and one of us would stay with him until some friends of his who worked in the Goodwill store could take him home later. Of course, I was the one who ended up staying with Harry out in the parking lot in front of the Goodwill store until they closed at about ten. So the two ladies took him back home.

Back when Harry got to work the next day, which happened to be on the weekend, I asked Harry how things had gone once he got home the night before, and he told me he had had another seizure. So I asked him if he had taken his medicine, and he told me no.

So I looked at Harry and I said, "If you don't take your medicine for me, then I am not going to do whatever you tell me to do for you." And that settled that, because from that day on, every time I saw him, I would ask him if he took his medicine, and then he was very good about taking it because he knew that I cared about him, and I knew that he also cared about me.

I mentioned that because there came a time when I was in a similar situation. There was a couple that needed a place to stay, and as I had done with David Johnson, I offered to rent them the spare room in my house. It just so happened that the young man also was an epileptic, and one night, he had a seizure, and his wife was scared to death and didn't know what to do. She was so afraid she thought he might die, but I knew what to do, so I told her to take a spoon and hold his tongue down until he passed out, but I told her once he woke up, he would be fine.

It just so happened that they were living with me around New Year's, so we all decided to have a party on New Year's Eve. Of course, the young man decided that he wanted to drink, so it fell to me that I could not drink, just in case he had another epileptic seizure, but luckily, everything went off without a hitch.

There are a couple more interesting stories about the time that I was living in that little house. One time, my phone would not work, so a gentleman showed up at my door to fix my telephone, and since I was still running my business out of my house, I needed the phone for business purposes. So he came and fixed my phone and then, for whatever reason, decided to sit down on my living room floor, and we started talking about the fact that a school was trying to pass a special levy. The levy was for the purpose of building a special school for only handicapped children, and as we got to talking about that, it reminded me of the way that I had been treated by the regular students when I attended Mount Logan School. As we talked, I told the repairman that in my opinion, that was not the correct way to go about dealing with handicapped students because if they were not allowed to deal with regular students, how were they to deal with the people whom they would meet as adults and throughout their everyday life? Because, as I told him, if the handicapped children were all kept by themselves, how were they going to be able to deal with things in their everyday lives once they became adults? And he thought for a minute, and then he said to me, "You are right. Having a special school just for handicapped kids is the wrong way to go about it." And I was further shocked by his next statement. He told me I should run for school board.

One day, out of the blue, my grandmother Maxine ended up at my house in Cincinnati, and she said she was coming to stay with me. I had no knowledge of her coming and did not even know she was on her way. When she arrived, she brought a dog. Of course, around that same time, my girlfriend, Barbara, decided to visit out of the blue, and I happened to be sick with a cold or the flu. Given the fact that I had one bedroom and my grandmother had the other bedroom, Barbara decided to stay because she said she was going to take care of me. That meant she ended up sleeping in the same bed with me, which I don't think my grandmother thought too much of, even though I was an adult and free to do as I wished. As things worked out, my grandmother didn't stick around very long because she knew that if Barbara was with me, I didn't need her around. Of course, I know my grandmother thought that Barbara and I were fooling around, but we never did anything physical. Even though it's hard to believe, our relationship was completely platonic. Of course, Barb didn't stick around long either, which was fine because, as I said earlier, even though I didn't know it at that time, God had other plans.

As I said earlier, not only did I do chair caning, but David Shaw, my partner, and I would also do some furniture refinishing. There was one thing I learned when being in business for myself, and that was that the customer is always right, even if I didn't think so. There was a situation when a lady called and told me that she had a dining room suite that she wanted refinished. She asked what David and I would charge her to refinish it. So we got together, drove to her house, and gave her a price for doing the job. Of course, that meant we had to rent a truck to pick up the dining room suite, take it to my house, and put it in the garage where we did furniture refinishing. It was dark wood, and she wanted a light fruitwood stain. So we started to strip down the dining room suite to remove the old stain. Once that was done, we had to try to find a light fruitwood stain, which was what the lady had wanted. After searching around for a few days, we finally found what she said she wanted. So we went ahead and refinished the furniture. When it was finished, we had to rent another truck to take the dining room suite back to her home. Originally, as I remember, the price we had given her was around two thousand dollars, but when we got to her house and were unloading the furniture, she looked at it and told both of us that she didn't like it and wasn't going to pay us the original agreed-to price. So by the time he and I had rented two trucks and figured in the cost of supplies, along with the fact that she did not pay the full price, we ended up only making about fifty dollars apiece on that job. But as I said, the customer is always right.

The last thing that I want to mention about living in that house was the fact that two girls who ended up being lesbians offered to paint my kitchen. Of course, they did what they promised, but in the process of doing so, they almost killed me. When they were done painting the kitchen, they decided they were going to dump the left-over paint down the kitchen sink. They got the brilliant idea that they were going to try to fix that problem by pouring bleach down the kitchen sink as well, which did not solve the problem because I ended up in the bathroom with my head stuck out the bathroom window, as the fumes from the bleach were burning my throat. For many years after that, I could not stand to smell regular bleach.

The last thing that I want to mention about living in Cincinnati was the time that I was able to go to a playoff game at Riverfront Stadium between the Cincinnati Reds and the Pittsburgh Pirates. I had bought tickets for that playoff game, which were seven rows from the top of the stadium in right field, which happened to be the position played by Roberto Clemente, who at that time was one of the best right fielders in the game of baseball. The two things that stand out to me about that game were one, the attendance for that game, which was 56,410 people, which I think was a record for Riverfront Stadium, and to my knowledge, that record was never broken. The other thing about that game that was unknown to any of us at that time was that it was the final game Roberto Clemente ever played because later that year, he was killed in a plane crash while en route to Nicaragua on a humanitarian mission to deliver supplies after a natural disaster.

My final thoughts for this chapter are about the gentleman from whom I rented the house. He decided to move to Florida, and after living down there for several years, he decided to sell the house. He then asked me if I would like to buy it, and I said I would like to try to buy it. But as it turned out, I was not able to buy it, and the person who bought it had me evicted. So once I had to move, I found another house in Glendale, but that was not a very nice house. So finally I decided to return to Chillicothe.

Chapter 4

From the time I was seventeen, when I went to Cincinnati for the first time, I had been living with my grandmother. Over the years, we had lived in many different homes that we rented. The first home that I lived in with my grandmother was the house on Vine Street, where we were living when I was still going to school at Mount Logan. But over the years, there were many other homes in which we lived. There was one home in which we lived that was not too far from the Mead paper mill. There were a couple of things about that house that brought back special memories for me. One memory had to do with one of my grandfather's other sisters, who I forgot to mention in the previous chapter. Her name was Esta Penrod Hawk. She was a wonderful lady, but one of the things that I liked was the fact that she worked at the Krispy Kreme Donuts shop, and every once in a while, Aunt Esta would stop by our house and drop off day-old donuts that they could not sell. This meant that my grandmother could have donuts with her coffee in the morning, or if I wanted something sweet and did not have any candy, I could just grab a couple of donuts to take care of my sweet tooth, which I still have today.

One of the other memories that I have about living in that house was the fact that it had a big backyard. I do not remember how or why, but while we were living in that house, I had gotten a rabbit cage and several rabbits. The cage was in the backyard of the house, so every day I would have to go out and feed the rabbits. But the funny thing about that was the fact that sometimes when I would try to feed the rabbits, they would be very calm and let me feed them, and sometimes they would give me a hard time and try to bite me when feeding them or cleaning their cages. There was one day when we were living at that house, my grandmother and I decided to take a ride because we were bored and did not have anything to do.

At that time, my grandmother owned a convertible, and that afternoon the sun was shining, and it was a very nice afternoon. Just around 3:00 p.m., we got in the car and headed up US 23 North, not knowing where we were going. Of course, when we decided to take a ride, we would just take off and then, as we went along, decide where to go. On this occasion, however, we had no particular destination in mind. As we continued driving up 23 North, all at once it started to rain, and since we had the top down, we had to pull off alongside the road and put the top up on the car. Then we took off again, and it started to rain even harder. The distributor cap got wet, and once that happened, we had to pull off the side of the road again because the car died. My grandmother had to get out of the car and raise the hood to dry off the distributor cap so that the car would start. Once we got back on the highway, we continued driving north. We finally got up to around Napoleon, Ohio, and we stopped to get something to eat. Once we ate, we took off again, and the next thing we knew, we were up around Toledo. Since we had gone that far, my grandmother asked if I wanted to go on up to Michigan and see Uncle Fred, and since it was not that much farther, I said yes. So we both decided that was what we were going to do. However, somehow we got turned around and didn't realize it, and as we drove, we realized that we were headed south on US 23. It must have been around 11:00 p.m. when we stopped at the McDonald's located near the Southern Shopping Center so that we could stretch our legs. When we got home and pulled into the yard, it was approximately three in the morning, so we had been gone for approximately twelve hours. So you can see, when we decided to do something on the spur of the moment, most of the time there was no plan, which also made it fun because we never knew where we were going or what we might run into in the process.

There was another time when my grandmother and I took another ride, and that was another time when we did not know where we were going. But on that occasion, we ended up in Greenup

County, Kentucky, and we stopped to stretch our legs. But we happened to stop in the parking lot of the Greenup County National Bank, and on that occasion, my grandmother happened to bring her camera. So she decided to take my picture standing in front of the bank. There were also many other things that the two of us used to do when we got tired of sitting at home. One was we used to go fishing at Paint Creek Lake. Once you parked your car in the parking lot, you could walk back this path next to the creek. There were several spots where you could get down to the water's edge, and I would usually sit in a folding chair with my fishing pole, and my grandmother would bait her hook and find a stick in the shape of a Y and take the handle of a fishing pole and stick one end of it in the dirt and put the other end of the pole and have it resting in the stick.

One time when we were fishing, I heard the fishing pole, and the end of it was bouncing up and down. Of course, she was not looking at it because she was busy doing something else. When she looked around, the bob wasn't doing anything. Then I looked over again, and it was doing the same thing. So once again, I told her, "You have a fish on your pole."

At that point, when she turned around, she saw the pole move and realized I was right. She began to reel it in and got it close to the bank. She was then trying to get the fish off the hook, but then she dropped the line and tried to pick it up again. As she was trying to take the fish off of the hook, she fell into the water and lost it, which was sort of funny at the time. When she realized I was laughing at her, she said to me, "That's not funny."

I said to her, "If you had seen it, you would have thought it was funny yourself." But the most important thing was that she was not hurt.

Whenever we did catch fish, there was a place where you could clean your fish. A lot of the time, there would be many people fishing, but they were catching carp, and they did not want them. So they would give them to my grandmother, and she would clean them and take them home. I like to fish, but I did not like to eat fish because of the bones.

When I was younger, there was a fish stand at the top of Yoctangee Park in Chillicothe, Ohio. For some reason, my mother and father decided to get a fish sandwich for me at the stand at the top of the park. On one occasion, they bought a sandwich for me. I happened to be sitting in the back of the car, and they had gone somewhere else, so I was in the car by myself. While I was eating the fish sandwich, I began to choke on what I thought was a bone in the fish. After trying several times to get the bone out, which was stuck in my throat, I have not eaten fish that has bones in it ever since. What made it worse for me was the fact that I was in the back seat of the car by myself, and my mom and dad were nowhere around.

Besides fishing, another thing that my grandmother and I used to do once in a while was going to the drive-in movie. At that time, there were two drive-ins in Chillicothe: the Torch Drive-In, located on US 23 South just on the outskirts of Chillicothe, and the other drive-in was the Fiesta Drive-In, which was located on US 23 North. There was one night when my grandmother and I went to the movies at the Fiesta. At that time, we were living in Pleasant Valley on Long Lane. On the way home, as we were driving through Pleasant Valley, we went under an underpass. As we got close to the underpass, it started to rain. So once again, we had to pull over and put the top up on the car because my grandmother still had the convertible.

The house we lived in in Pleasant Valley was very small, but it was also very nice. There was only one bedroom, so my grandmother slept in the bedroom, and I slept on the couch in the living room. When we were living there, we had a little dog named Pooch. He was not very big, and when he curled up, all you could see was a ball of fur. There was a store at the end of the lane, and sometimes when I would go to the mailbox, I would go to the store and see if I could buy candy. When we first moved there, they did not have red licorice, but I asked for it, so they started carrying it.

I remember one year while we were living there, it was the middle of December, and one day as I walked to the mailbox, the temperature was seventy degrees, and it did not even feel like winter. The people we were renting the house from, Mr. and Mrs. Long, were very nice people.

There came a time when my grandmother married a gentleman named Lawrence Copenhaver. He worked at the Eagles Lodge on

Douglas Avenue in Chillicothe, Ohio. He also helped out on bingo night at the Eagles. One night, when my grandmother and I went to bingo, there happened to be a lady sitting across the table from us. As the three of us got to talking, the fact that my birthday was coming up was mentioned. The lady sitting across the table then took a pen and a piece of paper out of her purse and started to write something. When she had finished writing, she handed it to me and wished me a happy birthday. Then she proceeded to tell us that she owned the Dairy Queen on High Street in Chillicothe. When I looked at the paper that she had given me, it stated I was entitled to several different kinds of ice cream, including regular ice cream bars or dilly bars and several other different kinds of ice cream.

One of the other things that I remember about the time my grandmother was married to Lawrence Copenhaver occurred one summer when I went to YMCA Camp. Because it was in town and it only occurred during the day, I ended up staying with my grandmother and Lawrence at his house. One afternoon, I had gotten home from camp, and my grandmother was not there yet. While I was waiting for her to come home, I was talking to Lawrence about my day at camp.

A little while later, my grandmother returned home. She had been out shopping, and when she got home, he asked her where she had been and accused her of being with another man. She said she had been shopping and had done nothing else. Then he started arguing with her. The more he argued, the madder he got. All at once, he grabbed her by the hair of the head and started to drag her upstairs, and she was screaming for him to stop. All this time, I was sitting on the couch watching the whole thing. As he started up the stairs, I felt pretty sure that he was going to take her upstairs and beat her, and I made up my mind that I was not going to let him do that to my grandmother. I then told him that if he did not stop, I was going to call the police, but I also told him that I wanted to kill him, so he let her go. I told him that I would not let anyone hurt my grandmother. When he walked to the bathroom, I got up and followed him. When we went into the bathroom, he apologized to me and told me he was sorry, but I told him I accepted his apology, but I still hated him. That was the last thing that I remember because shortly thereafter, they got divorced. I do not know why they got married in the first place.

As I mentioned earlier in this chapter, there was one time when my grandmother and I lived in a house that my mom and dad had bought on Black Run Road. When we lived in that house, my grandmother's brother, Raymond, was diagnosed with cancer of the voice box and had to have his voice box removed. He had a hole in his throat and used a device that vibrated when he held it next to his throat so that you could try to understand what he was saying. My grandmother used to have to go down to his trailer every day to help him around his house. His other sister, Nina Jean, lived close by as well. But as time went on, my grandmother's brother Raymond, who we all liked, saw his health begin to deteriorate. At one point, he moved in with his sister, Nina Jean, and her family. She had several children: a girl named Vicky and another girl whose name I cannot recall, as well as two sons, one named David and the other named Danny. When we lived on Black Run Road, there were several times when Danny would stop by to see if we needed anything. There was one particular winter day when he did so. He asked if we needed anything, and we told him no, but there had been a big snowstorm. So while Danny was there, he decided to build a snowman.

As I said before, my mother and dad always seemed to find a house that they could buy and remodel. Our house on Black Run Road, like many others before it, had an outhouse. I know that my mother had done some remodeling on that house by putting in a drop ceiling, which had a metal frame, and I think there were ceiling tile pieces that went in each section of the metal frame. There was one day when my grandmother's brother came to visit, and my mother happened to be there working on the drop ceiling when, all at once, part of the ceiling fell down and hit him in the head. Luckily, he was not hurt, but my mother had to redo that part of the ceiling.

As time went on, my grandmother's brother, as I said, was living with Nina Jean and her family, but one day my grandmother found out that he wanted to come to our house. So she went to Nina's to pick him up. When they got ready to leave to come back to our house, Nina's kids told him they would see him later, and he said to them, "No, you will not." But little did any of us know what was to come because later that night, he had tried to go to bed in my room, so I ended up sleeping in my grandmother's room. But several times that evening, he would get up and go and open the front door and look out. When he would look out, he would look up. This happened several times, and my grandmother later told me what was about to happen. She would have stayed up with him because when we woke up the next morning, we realized that he had passed away during the night. And to my knowledge, I do not know how much more work, if any, my mother and dad did on that house.

Shortly thereafter, my grandmother and I moved to a house on Rozelle Creek Road that my mom and dad still owned, even though by that time, they had purchased Huntington Grocery located on the corner of Blain Highway and State Route 772. There was one good thing about living on Rozelle Creek Road: when I got bored and did not have anything to do, I could take off and walk from the house we were living to the store to see my mother. It's about a mile or maybe a little more from the house on the hill to the store. Sometimes, it would be around two in the afternoon when I would decide to walk to the store. There was a lady named Marion Milner who lived in a two-story house on State Route 772, and a lot of the time when I was walking to the store, she would either be walking to the store or back from the store after picking up her *Chillicothe Gazette*.

There came a time when my grandmother decided to go to Florida. When she decided to go to Florida, I wanted to stay in the house by myself. So I went into the Ross County Welfare Department and asked if they would help me so I could stay in the house. Of course, they told me no, so I ended up having to move down with my mom and dad and my sister, Tracy, on the back of the store. There was enough room for all of us. My sister Tracey had a black poodle named FeFe.

There were three bedrooms in the living quarters. While I was living there, I would help out on delivery day, which was every Tuesday. I would help stock the shelves and do anything else I was asked to do. I had my own television in my room, so I could watch my baseball games and not disturb anyone else.

While I was living there, I was collecting baseball cards. Every week or so, I would have my mother order a box of baseball cards that had bubblegum in them. Of course, I was paying for the cards because I didn't want to get them for free, as I found it wouldn't be fair. I was comfortable while living there and could eat anything I wanted that was in the store.

There came a point in time when living in the store became very handy because, in the winter of 1978 and 1979, we had an old-fashioned blizzard. We had so much snow that the roads became impassable, and even though the store was located on the corner of Blain Highway and State Route 772, it became impossible for some people to even get to the store to get what they needed. Even though we lived at the store, we could not get out the back door due to the snow being piled up to the window. So if we wanted to go out, we had to go out the front door of the store. That year, we had so much snow that the National Guard was called in to clear the snow off of the highway, and my father was even asked by Franklin Conaway if he would use his dozer to help clear the snow off of the highway, which he did. And to my knowledge, that was the only time that a private citizen was asked or was allowed to run his own equipment on the highway, but that shows how bad and how much snow we had in Ross County the winter of 1978–1979.

Chapter 5

My grandmother finally returned from Florida. One day, when we were out taking a ride, we were driving on State Route 159 when we noticed an empty mobile home sitting in an empty parking lot. There was no one around it, and I cannot remember whether there was a phone number or name to call on it for information, but somehow my grandmother ended up finding out who owned it and how much they wanted for it.

As I said in the previous chapter, at one time, my grandmother and I had lived in my mother and father's house, which they lived in before they bought Huntington Grocery on State Route 772. There was some property just down the hill from the house, so my mother and father gave us permission to put our mobile home on that piece of property. But before the mobile home could be brought in and set up, my father had to put in a septic tank. Once that was done, they came to deliver our mobile home. When they came with it, they set it up. I think the guys had been drinking because there were beer bottles all over the place, and I also think it was possible that they may have been drinking before they got there because the mobile home was not leveled up correctly. One end of it was buried in the dirt, and the other end was about two and a half to three feet off the ground. The end that was buried in the dirt did not have any blocks under it, and the other end had two sets of blocks about three or four high. For some reason, the guys had to come back the next day to finish the job, but my grandmother told them not to bring any more beer with them.

After that, we had to try to put skirting around the bottom of the mobile home, which was not easy because the mobile home was not level. So each piece of skirting was a different height, and you had to cut them one piece at a time. There was a plastic track that you put in the ground with spikes. One end of the skirting would go in the tracks, and the other end would go up underneath the edge of the mobile home. That was supposed to help hold the top of the skirting in place. Sometimes it worked, and sometimes it didn't. If it was windy, sometimes the skirting would blow off, and you would have to walk around the yard trying to find it. There were several times during the winter when we lived there when our water lines would freeze up. At those times, my dad would have to bring up a giant gas heater. Then he would have to take off a piece of the skirting so he could use the heater to thaw out the water lines. This occurred on several different occasions.

There were other things that we had to do when we owned the mobile home. When we first bought it, we had to fix one issue: it had crank-out windows, and when it used to rain, they would leak like sieves because you could not shut the windows tight enough to keep the rain from coming in. There was a place called Damon's, which was located on US 23 South just north of Waverly, Ohio. It was a place where you could find almost anything you wanted or needed as far as used trailer parts were concerned. My grandmother and I went down there and found some new windows for our mobile home that raised up and down instead of cranking in and out. Of course, they still leaked when it rained, but not as bad as the first set of windows.

In the summertime, the mobile home would get very hot, and the only way we had of keeping cool was to either open the windows or use one small rotating fan that we would set in the middle of the living room floor.

The other thing about living in the mobile home was that it was very cold in the winter and hard to heat. One year, my grandmother and I went to Oliver's General Store and bought a stove to put in the living room of our mobile home. The difficult thing about the stove that we had in the living room was that since there was no chimney, we had to stick a stovepipe out of one of the windows on the back side of the mobile home, with an elbow on the end of it and another pipe that went straight up into the air. Since you could burn either coal or wood in the stove, you would have to empty out the ashes about every other day. But we only used the stove for one winter because one morning when we woke up, the part of the stovepipe that stuck straight out of the window was still there, but the elbow with the other piece of pipe on it had come off and was laying down over the hill in our backyard. Also, there was the fact that our mobile home had wood paneling in every room, but the paneling behind the stove in the living room would get very hot and could have easily caught on fire, so we decided to do away with the stove.

Our mobile home also had a gas furnace, which we decided to use even though propane was more expensive. We had a five-hundred-gallon tank that we had gotten from Litters in Chillicothe. We had to have the tank filled about two and a half times every year. It usually cost between five hundred and six hundred dollars a year, which I suppose was not too bad.

One of the other things that I remember about living in the mobile home was that we had a fenced-in yard, and my grandmother and I had a dog named Fluffy. After we had lived in the mobile home for a short time, my mother and father, who still owned Huntington Grocery, had a cat named Ginger. Because the store was along 772, my mother was afraid that Ginger would get hit if she got out, so she decided to give Ginger to my grandmother and me. So then we had a dog and a cat. But the strange thing is that as time went on, Fluffy began to only eat cat food because I think she thought she was a cat. If you bought her dog food, she would not eat it. Another of the strange things that Fluffy would do was that she would let you know when she wanted to go outside, and when she wanted to come in, she would scratch on the door to let you know that she was there.

Sometimes, the two of them would get to wrestling around, and since Fluffy had long hair, Ginger's claws would get caught in it. Then my grandmother and I would have to separate them. But Ginger had another bad habit: there was a hole in our front yard where a mother rabbit used to have her babies, and if Ginger realized the babies were there, she would try to kill them. So my grandmother would have to chase her with a newspaper to keep her from killing them. Another bad habit she had was that she used to bring live mice into the house because she wanted to play with them before she killed them.

In my room, I only had a twin bed, but every night when it was time to go to bed, there would be me, Fluffy, and Ginger, all sleeping in a twin bed. Fluffy would either sleep beside me or between my legs, and Ginger usually slept at or on my feet. So once again, I feel it may have been another example of the fact that Fluffy and Ginger may have known that they were supposed to watch out for me.

As time went on, my grandmother and I began to plant different types of trees. We had ordered some trees out of a gardening magazine. I had ordered three evergreen trees and either three or four cherry trees. There was a walnut tree behind our mobile home, and every year in the fall, you could hear the walnuts fall off the tree because they would hit the top of the mobile home. When they would first fall off the tree, they would have a green outer shell on them, so we would have to pick them up and lay them in the driveway. Then, as we would drive over them with the car, the green shells would fall off, and you could pick up the walnuts. Luckily, they were black walnuts, which are sometimes very hard to find around this area. But I can remember for many years seeing my dad take one of the black walnuts, take a hammer to crack it, and then you would have to pick the nuts out of the shells before you could eat them. Two of the three evergreen trees I purchased eventually died, and only one lived. The one that lived happened to be in the front yard. Eventually, it became big enough that we could finally put lights on it and decorate it for Christmas. As for my cherry trees, I think only two of the three survived, but they both had cherries on them. However, the one that was behind our mobile home, down over the hill, was the biggest because it got all of the water that ran out of our septic tank.

As time went on and my grandmother and I settled into our life at the mobile home, there were still times in the spring of the year when my grandmother would go to Hirsch Fruit Farm, which was located on State Route 772. Every spring, when it was time, she would go and pick strawberries. If you picked your own, they were cheaper than if you bought them there. Then she would bring them home, clean them, cut them up, and put them in freezer containers for winter. For several years, we also used to can our own sauerkraut. Ruby Gragg, one of my grandmother's other sisters, and her husband, Bill, would give us some of the biggest heads of cabbage I had ever seen. Bill had a cabbage cutter, which he would loan to us, so we would cut up the cabbage, and we had an old stone crock in which we would put water and salt. Then we would put in the cabbage that we had cut up, and then we would put a plate on top of it and weight it down with a brick or a rock. It would stay in the crock for a couple of weeks, and once it had fermented, then we would put it in canning jars. Sometimes the smell would take your breath away, but it would taste awful good during the winter. We also used to buy corn on the cob, then we would cut it off the cob, put it in containers, and put it in the freezer for winter as well. We also used to make our own hamburger relish. We would grind the vegetables for it with a grinder that you could fasten to the counter, but you had to crank it by hand.

So as you can see, even though many years had passed, some things stayed the same. As time went on, my mother and father decided to sell Huntington Grocery. Before they sold it, they decided to build a new house on top of the hill on Rozelle Creek Road. The house was big, with a huge living room, big dining room, three bedrooms, and two bathrooms upstairs, and one in the basement. It also had an in-ground swimming pool.

There came a time when my uncle Wayne, his wife, Marilyn, and their four boys, Brian, David, Dale, and Scottie, moved to Ohio so my uncle Wayne could find work. My cousin Mike Penrod, who is a brother to my uncle Wayne, as I mentioned in a previous chapter, was a painter and worked for a company out of Columbus, Ohio. My uncle Wayne was able to get on and work for the company my cousin Mike worked for. At that point, there were seven people living in our mobile home. At that point, I decided to go to my mother and father's house to live because there was not enough room for all of us in the mobile home and the fact that Marilyn was expecting another baby.

On several occasions, while they were living with us, they had to make several trips down to Florida to make sure the things that they had left there were still okay. One of the things I remember about the first trip was when Dale was small. When we would be driving down the road and we would pass a McDonald's, Dale would never miss one, but he could not say "McDonald's"; he would say, "Dad, there's a Donald's."

When we got to Florida, everything was just as they had left it. So then we returned to Ohio. I also made a second trip to Florida with them, and everything was fine the second time as well, except when we returned to Ohio this time, they came back up Interstate 95 through North and South Carolina, Virginia, and West Virginia. One night it was snowing, and we had to stop at a hotel room that had a very small square bathtub. As we came back to Ohio, there was a lot of snow, and the one thing I remember the most was that we were driving through the mountains, and there were a lot of ramps along the highway for the semitrucks to be able to stop in bad weather and not run off the side of the mountain.

As it got close to Christmas that year, we were able to put lights on the Christmas tree in the front yard. I remember that my grandmother took the doorknob out of the kitchen door so we could run an extension cord outside to be able to plug in the Christmas lights on the tree. The other thing that I remember about that year was that we had cement blocks for steps to get out of the kitchen door. When Marilyn started out the kitchen door and slipped and fell, she broke her tailbone. Luckily, she was not seriously injured, but she was also pregnant with their last son, Marcus.

So for almost the next year, I lived at my mother and father's house, sleeping on a mattress in the living room behind their couch. At the same time, Connie was expecting my niece, Christina. When Christina came home from the hospital, she lived at the house with my mom and dad. Over the next year, as she grew up, I still remember as though it were yesterday. Almost every day, when Christina would come into the living room, she would be carrying a handful of storybooks. She would look at me and say, "Read." At that point, I would have to stop whatever I was doing and read to her.

My uncle Wayne, his wife, Marilyn, and their four boys were finally able to return to their home in Florida. Once that occurred, I was able to return to our mobile home, and everything returned to normal. However, I must say that the situation did give my grandmother the opportunity to spend time with her other grandchildren.

Several years before, my grandmother and I had flown to Florida to spend Thanksgiving with my uncle Wayne, Marilyn, Brian, Scottie, and David, which were the three boys that they had at that time. At that time, they lived in the city of Jacksonville. The house in which they lived was very close to the Gator Bowl. I remember when we decided to take the trip to Florida, I had never been on an airplane. But I still remember we flew at night, and I remember going to the airport in Columbus, Ohio. That night stands out in my memory for several reasons. One was the fact that I had on a shirt that looked like a Hawaiian shirt, which happened to have short sleeves.

As we got to the airport in Columbus and prepared to check in for our flight, the passengers had to go through metal detectors, which my grandmother also did. But I could not because of my crutches, which were metal, so a lady had to use a handheld device to check me since I could not go through the regular way. At that point, you still had to walk outside across the tarmac and walk up a flight of stairs, which was on wheels and rolled up to the airplane. As we were walking across the tarmac, I realized how cold I was with my short-sleeved shirt on. As I got to the bottom of the steps and looked up, I thought to myself, *Do I really want to do this?* Once I had made my way to the top of the steps, I stepped inside the airplane, and my grandmother and I then took our seats. As we were sitting there waiting to take off, the pilot came over the intercom and said we had a ten-minute flight to Dayton, Ohio. As the plane began to take flight, and I knew we were in the air, I was fine, except I thought that my stomach was still on the ground. Then shortly after, we landed in Dayton to pick up some other passengers. We were flying in a DC-9 or DC-10, and then our next stop was in Atlanta, Georgia. Thankfully, we did not have to change planes but had a short layover. Once we took off from Atlanta, it was a short flight to Jacksonville, Florida. As I had mentioned earlier, when we left Columbus, Ohio, I was wearing that short-sleeved shirt, and it had been chilly, but by the time we had gotten to Jacksonville and had gotten off the plane, it was seventy-two degrees, even though it was around 10:00 p.m. So I ended up wearing the right shirt after all.

There was no dirt around Wayne and Marilyn's house; it was all sand, and the yard was full of sand spurs. If you stayed outside very long, they would bite you. And I got bitten quite a lot, but it was not because I was outside a lot; it was because I did not walk very fast, so they had a better chance to bite me. One day, when I was outside walking around, I pulled a groin muscle, and from that point on, I had a very difficult time walking. And I was sleeping on the couch in their living room, and one morning I woke up, and Wayne and Marilyn were arguing about something. Since I had pulled that groin muscle, I was not feeling very well. But I decided to take a walk to do some thinking, and I told my grandmother that if they were going to continue fighting, I did not want to stay. I told her I would ride a bus home, and she could stay. I don't know if they realized that I was upset, but they stopped fighting, so I decided to stay for the rest of our visit. I remember when we went to the airport in Jacksonville, we were on a 737 jet. I remember that it had big seats, and you had a lot of room, and they served us Coke and peanuts on the flight to Atlanta, where we had to change planes. But in Atlanta, you could walk right off the plane and right into the airport. But of course, once again, we were on a DC-10, which was like being in a tin can after flying from Jacksonville to Atlanta on the 737. Once we got back to Columbus, Ohio, we were then able to drive back to Chillicothe. And even though we enjoyed the trip, it felt very good to be home again. So far, that is the only flight I have ever taken on an airplane.

It was sometime later that I became acquainted with a young lady by the name of Patty Schrake. She was a very nice young lady who worked with some of the students at Pioneer School. The two of us began dating. We did many different things. There would be times we would go to the drive-in movies at the Fiesta or the Torch, which were the two drive-in movie theaters that I had mentioned earlier. There were some occasions when the two of us would serve as chaperones for some of the activities for the students at Pioneer School. There was one occasion when the two of us had to go to the Valley House Restaurant, for which both of us had to dress up. She wore a nice dress, and I had to wear a suit. Two of the students she worked with were Bud and Cindy McQuay. Both of them happened to be in wheelchairs. Their parents' names were Clyde and Donna McQuay, who were very nice people. They had three other children, and their names were Ralph, Junior, and Tammy.

On some weekends, when we did not have anything else to do, Patty and I would go to Clyde and Donna's and play games. Bud and Cindy always seemed to like that because they would roll their wheelchairs into the kitchen so they could watch us play games. There was another time when I was taking classes to get my GED. I was taking the classes at the Carver Community Center, and one day, Patty told me that a friend of hers, who taught a preschool class there as well, wanted the two of us to talk to the children about what it was like to be handicapped. So, of course, we agreed to do it. The name of the lady who taught the class was Marjorie McIntyre. So one afternoon after I had finished my class, Patty and I went into Marjorie's classroom. The two of us did our best to answer any and all of the questions the children asked about what it was like to be handicapped. There was one other thing that happened while the two of us were dating. We became involved as volunteers with the March of Dimes and participated in several of their fundraising events. But one night, when Patty and I had gone out on a date and she was dropping me off at home, she told me she had something she needed to talk to me about. As we were sitting in her car in my driveway, she told me that she was breaking up with me, but she did not tell me why. So I got out of the car and walked into the house, not knowing what had happened, and she drove away.

I was very upset and hurt by what had happened. Luckily, I had a neighbor who lived across the road, whose name was Sandy Vandemark. There were times that she and I would talk to each other, trying to figure out what had happened, but I could not come up with an answer. Eventually, I was in Yoctangee Park in Chillicothe on a fundraiser for the March of Dimes, and it just so happened that I ran into Patty. Finally, I cornered her and forced her to give me an answer as to why we had split up. She then told me that her parents had told her that if she married me, they would write her out of their will. But the strange thing about that was the fact that neither one of her parents had ever met me, which I thought was kind of unfair because the Bible says, "Judge not, lest ye be judged," and I was being judged by people who had never met me or, as far as I knew, did not know anything about me or the type of person that I was. As the Bible says, we should not judge each other unfairly when there may be things that we do not know about that person or their situation. As the Bible says, we should love our neighbors as ourselves and do unto others as you would have them do unto you. If you do not know about a person's situation, then do not unfairly judge them because God is the final judge of every person and every situation. And as I had previously stated, God had a greater plan for my life, as I would find out later.

Chapter 6

Shortly after Patty Schrake and I broke up, I began to think that if I was going to spend the rest of my life by myself, I had to decide what I wanted to do. Even though I was still living with my grandmother, it was different because she was getting older, and I did not have anyone to go places or do things with. But then, for some reason, I ran into a young man whose name was John Rhodes. He may have been about my age or maybe a little bit younger, but we soon found that we both liked to do the same things. As time went on, he began to come out to my house, and even though we did not do anything at my house, I think my grandmother wondered what in the world we were going to do. Because he would come out to my house and ask me if I wanted to take a ride, and most of the time, I would say yes, and he would get in his car and take off. Of course, it was somewhat similar to my grandmother's and my situation years before, for a lot of the times when we would take off, we didn't know where we were going or what we were going to do.

John owned a red Plymouth Duster with a black vinyl top. John had a family, but his wife was a lot younger than he was. His wife's name was Lori, but she was only seventeen years old, but they had the cutest little boy I had ever seen, but I cannot remember his name. There were times when we would go to John's house. His mother and father lived back a lane just as you came to the bottom of Cabbage Patch Hill, which then turns into the US 50 East. As you got to the bottom of the hill, John's family lived in a mobile home, and John's grandmother lived in the house next door. John's parents and grandmother were very nice people, and when I got to visit them, it was the first time that I also met John's wife, Lori, and his little boy. I feel like John was the person that I needed in my life at the time because when I was with him, we were always out doing something, which kept me from thinking about the breakup. I had because it felt like I was thirty or in my early thirties, which made me start thinking about having to spend my life alone if something happened to my grandmother. But even as I was going through the things that I was going through, God had plans, even though I was not aware of them, because, as I've said several times before, God knows what is ahead of each and every one of us, and he has a plan for each and every one of us, even though we cannot see it or we may not understand it.

There was one time when John came to my house, and he asked if I wanted to take a ride, and of course, I said yes because I wanted to get out of the house. Of course, my grandmother asked where we were going, and I said I didn't know. Then she asked when we would be back, and of course, I said I didn't know that either. I just told her we would be back later. One time, we were heading up US 23 North. We were stopped at a traffic light that was close to the DuPont plant. As we were sitting at the light waiting for it to change, another car pulled up in the other lane and started racing its engine. As John and I were waiting for the light to change, we looked at each other and said, "I think he wants to race," and John asked me if I thought we could beat him, and I said I did not know, but we could find out. As I said, John owned a red Plymouth Duster with a black vinyl top that would absolutely fly. As the traffic light changed, John hit the gas, and we left the other car sitting in the dust. John and I went on to Columbus. As we were headed back toward Chillicothe before we got to Scioto Downs, John asked me if I wanted to stop, and I told him if he wanted to, it was okay with me. So we decided to stop. As we went in, we bought a racing program and found a horse that looked kind of interesting, so I made a two-dollar bet. That was the only race I bet on. A little while later, we decided to leave and headed home. I do not remember whether or not I told my grandmother that we had stopped at Scioto Downs. Then one day, John came to the house and asked me if I wanted to go fishing, and I said yes. So the two of us drove to Paint Creek. We had to stop and pick up some bait. Once we parked the car in the parking lot, we started walking back the path and decided to walk all the way around to the other side of the dam, which meant we had to go up one set of steps, across, and then down another set of steps on the other side. There had been a fence around that part of the walkway, but someone had removed part of the fence, and it was open. So the two of us sat down and let our feet hang over the dam, and since it was late in the evening, we decided to go ahead and fish all night. At one point, the two of us must have fallen asleep because when we woke up, it had started to rain, and since there was no cover, we could not stay where we were, so we had to walk back up the steps, down, and all the way back to the parking lot in the rain. Once we got to John's car, we went back to sleep. Later, when we woke up again, John was trying to do something with his fishing pole, and somehow he had hurt his hand, and it had started bleeding. So we had to drive back to the house of John's parents so he could work on the injury to his hand. You see, John and I did a lot of different things and had a lot of fun together.

One day, John came by the house. He told me that he, his wife, Lori, and their little boy were going to take a trip to Terre Haute, Indiana, where Laurie's mother lived. He asked me if I wanted to go along. Since I really had no reason not to and had nothing to keep me in Chillicothe, I decided to go along. Once we got there, I was able to meet Lori's mother, and she seemed to be a very nice lady. But I also got to meet a friend of John's who was a young man who had been friends with John for a long time. So the first evening we were there, Lori, John, and I decided to go to a taco place to get something to eat. When we ordered our food, I realized that they had three different taco salsas: hot, hotter, and extra hot. As John, Lori, and I ordered our food, John and I decided to get the hottest one they had. John's friend did not realize what we were doing because we did not tell him we had ordered the hottest one they had, so he ordered the same thing as John and I. Of course, back then, I had a cast-iron stomach and could eat anything that I wanted, and it didn't bother me at all. As we were all sitting there eating, John's friend realized how hot they were and began to drink everything he could get his hands on. He looked at us and said, "Are you trying to set me on fire?" and John and I said, "No, we didn't tell you to order the same thing we did." So we went home that night back to the house of Lori's mother and went to bed.

The next day, when we got up, John decided he wanted to go to the auto parts store and get some cherry bombs to put on his car. So the two of us went to pick out what he wanted. He got the tools out and started working on the car. Of course, he had to take something off of the car because the cherry bomb was fastened to the side of the engine, and there was a cherry bomb on each side. There came a point when John was having a problem holding one of the parts while he was trying to bolt it to the engine. As he was having a problem, I told him to give me a minute, and then I would help him. So I got down on my hands and knees and crawled under the car while we put the bolts in.

Later that evening, Lori, John, and I decided to take a ride to try out the car, and John's friend went along as well. We came to a point on the highway where there was this great stretch, and we had stopped. John's friend and Lori were sitting in the backseat. I looked at John, and he looked at me, but neither one of us said a word to each other. But both of us knew what the other one was thinking. Then John floored it, and when I looked at the speedometer, we were going anywhere between 100 and 110 down the straight stretch of highway. John's wife, Lori, didn't, but John's friend, who was sitting behind me, all I could see was the whites of his eyes, and he looked like he was scared to death. After that, we drove at normal speed down the highway. I don't know which one it was, but John or Lori noticed that there was a marijuana plant growing along the road, so they decided to stop and pick it up. But before we got back to the house of Lori's mother, John stopped at a liquor store and bought a couple of small bottles of liquor to soak their marijuana in so they could smoke it. While they were doing their thing, John asked me if I wanted to try it, and I said no because I have enough problems without doing something like that. So there are certain things that I would do under no circumstances.

The night before we went to bed, there had been a little alcohol left in the little bottles that John had purchased. I don't know why, but he decided to give some to the dog of Lori's mother, and there must have been enough left to make the dog a little tipsy. There were a lot of rocks in Terre Haute, Indiana. We just drove around so John could let me see some of them, and he also said that people used to swim in them, which I know is true because there was a movie in which these boys went swimming in one of those stone quarries.

At one point, while I was in Terre Haute, Indiana, John and I were talking, and I don't know how the subject came up, but we were talking about going back to school. So he suggested that I might want to check out Indiana State University, which I decided to do. So he drove me to the campus, and I did talk to an advisor. While I was there, we discussed several different things, and I told her that I would think about it.

One night, John and I, along with Lori's mother and John's friend, decided to go out to a bar. Since John's wife was seventeen, she was not old enough to go, so she had to stay home and babysit. The four of us went out. When we got there, we were sitting and talking while we were drinking. John met a couple of other friends he knew at the bar. As time passed and we were sitting and talking and enjoying ourselves, there were some people who came into the bar, and as I remember, I think they wanted to start fighting with the friend of John's whom I had met on the first night we got to Terre Haute, Indiana. It was getting late, so the four of us decided to leave and go get something to eat. So we ended up stopping at the Waffle House. John, Lori's mother, and I ordered what we wanted to eat. However, John was in the restroom at the restaurant. We thought he was getting sick from drinking too much at the bar. Once we had finished eating, we took John's friend home and then went back to the house of Lori's mother and went to bed. When John and I got up the next morning, we went to check on his friend to see if he was okay, and he was fine. As things turned out, I realized that John and Lori intended to stay longer, and I had decided not to attend Indiana State University, so I had no further reason to stay. So I bought a ticket and rode a Greyhound bus back to Chillicothe. I only saw John one other time, and it was many years later. See, that was another time when God put someone in my life that I needed to help me deal with the breakup with Patty and my fear of being alone if something ever happened to my grandmother. But once again, I say that God had other plans, as He always does.

Chapter 7

This chapter will discuss several different things. One is about a visit that my mother and I made to my dad's brother and sister-in-law, Gary and Sherry Blazer. They lived on Poplar Street in Chillicothe, Ohio, which happened to be a one-way street, which is a very important factor in the next part of my story. My mother and I stopped to visit them, but my uncle Gary was not home at the time, so my mother and I visited with my aunt Sherry and their three boys, Gary Jr., Jerry, and Terry.

After visiting for a while, my mother said she was almost ready to leave, so she told me I could go ahead and go out and get in the car, and she would be out in a few minutes. So I did as she said. The passenger side of the car was out in the street. As I opened the door and put my crutches in the back seat and started to get in, the door accidentally knocked me down as it closed. While I was lying in the street, I looked up, and there was a street sweeper coming straight at me. I got up and once again tried to open the door, but once again, the door closed and knocked me down a second time. Once again, I looked, and the street sweeper was still coming. I opened the door a third time and remember getting in the car, but when the street sweeper went by, I went to the driver who was driving it as he drove past me because I was sitting in the car with the door shut. While this was happening, my mother had not yet come out of the house to get in the car to go home. And to the best of my memory, I do not think I ever told her what had happened. So that was another time when God was watching out for and taking care of me.

On December 25, 1971, my grandfather, Virgil Penrod, passed away. On the evening of December 25, that evening, my mother and father got a phone call that my grandfather was not well, so they had to leave and drive to Knockemstiff. They were still living in the house on Rozelle Creek Road that we had moved into in the mid-1960s. When they left, they told me I could call Carol and Kathy Sutherland to come down and stay with me while they were gone. And the other thing about that night was that I called my grandmother Maxine to tell her what was going on, so I think she went out to check out everything and to check on what was happening with my grandfather. When Carol and Kathy came down, the three of us were playing pool on the pool table we had in the living room of our house. As we were playing and I was walking around the pool table, I think I slipped and fell, and then Red fell on top of me and landed on my leg. The two of us have a running joke where I said she tried to break my leg because she said I was cheating in pool. I told her it was my pool table and it was in my house, but she said that didn't make any difference; I was still cheating. That was one good memory that occurred on a night when I lost my grandfather, who I loved very much, and I have always wondered if my grandfather had time to ask God, "Can you say it to him?" before he died.

I believe that was when I went to stay with my grandmother once again when we were living in the house in Pleasant Valley. That was the house that only had one bedroom, so my grandmother slept in the bedroom, and I slept on the couch. I still remember to this day the fact that I did not cry about my grandfather's passing until the day of his funeral. They had his body at the house where they lived placed in front of the picture window across from Shady Glen Church in Knockemstiff. As I said, I had not cried prior to the time that they took his body out of the house to carry it across the road to the church where his funeral service was held. My mother told me I could not go to the funeral, so when they carried his body out of the house, it hit me that I would never see him again, at least on earth. As I was sitting there weeping, my grandfather's brother, my uncle Fred, walked up to me and told me it would be alright, and I do not know why, but he folded up some money and put it in my hand, and then, as I remember, he went on over to the church for the funeral.

There was something else that happened in that house. My uncle Ernest Penrod, whom we called Bob, lived in that house with his wife, Priscilla, whom we called Sill. She had a son named Max from a previous marriage. Her son Max used to come to visit her every once in a while when he was out of the service and on furlough. I can remember seeing him in his uniform when he would come to visit his mother. There is one thing that I will mention here that I did not find out until many years later, that Max's last name was Elliot. Max has since passed away, but sometimes it is strange how things seem to come full circle. And that is because the church that my wife and I now attend, the First Free Will Baptist Church, is the church that Max's wife, Charlotte, still attends on occasion.

Several years ago, we were having a baptismal service at a creek, and Max's wife, Charlotte, was present. She started to talk to me about the past. She remembered me from when I was a little boy and visiting my grandfather in Knockemstiff. That is why I say it seems like things come full circle.

The other thing that I remember was when my grandmother and I were living in the house on Vine Street. My uncle Bob came to visit and stayed for a little while, maybe an hour or so, and he said he had to head home because it was getting late and Sill would have supper ready. When my uncle Bob got home that afternoon, Sill had gone to the bathroom and had asked my uncle Bob to stir a pan of fried potatoes that were cooking on the stove. As he got up to do what she asked, he must have had a heart attack because when she came back to the kitchen, he was lying on the kitchen floor, and from what I understand, he must have already been dead. Both my grandfather and my uncle Bob were fifty-nine years of age at the time of their deaths. My aunt Ruby, who they called Tootie, was fifty-eight years old at the time of her death, but the doctors told the family that she had the body of an eighty-year-old woman. My uncle Floyd, who they called Bud, was around sixty or sixty-one years old at the time of his death. My uncle Bud was being taken to the hospital in the backseat of an automobile. My aunt Jane was sitting in the backseat of the automobile with my uncle Bud's head in her lap. I am not sure whether he passed away before or after they reached the hospital. I don't know if any of them had a chance to ask God to save them before they died or not. I believe that those of us who are Christians have that blessed assurance to know that we have a heavenly home waiting for us, but if anyone, including myself, does not know whether or not some of our family members made it to heaven, we will not know that answer until we get there ourselves. But the wonderful thing is that if our loved ones are there, we will know them there as we knew them here. If they are not there, we will not remember that because it would be too painful, and it says in the Bible that there will be no sickness or pain of any kind in heaven.

Chapter 8

This chapter begins to tell the rest of my story. My grandmother and I were still living in our mobile home on Rozelle Creek when I decided to buy a satellite dish. Little did I know that the satellite dish would play such an important part in my future. On Sunday, May 27, 1987, I was sitting in my bedroom watching television. That Sunday morning, I happened to turn on a church program, and as I was watching it, the Holy Spirit spoke to me and let me know that I needed to get saved that very day, which also happened to be the last Sunday of revival at Pleasant Valley Plug Run Church of Christ in Christian Union. My mother had previously asked me to go to the revival with her that evening.

When she picked me up that evening, as we drove to the revival, I was still thinking about what had happened earlier that day as I was watching the church program on television. As we got to the church that evening, I remember I was sitting in the next-to-last row in the back of the church. As the service began, I realized that the Holy Spirit once again was speaking to me about what I needed to do. It was then that I got up out of my seat and proceeded down the aisle toward the altar. As I was walking, I was also weeping, and as I got to the altar, I began to pray and ask the Lord to forgive me for all my sins. At that point, I knew there had been a change because I felt totally different inside, and I knew that God had forgiven me of all the mistakes and sins that I had committed in my life.

When I got up from the altar, I knew that my life had a new beginning, or I would say, I was a brand-new creature in Christ Jesus. But little did I know how much more wonderful my life would be once I gave my life to Him. And now I look back and wonder why I waited so long and wasted so many years because I thought I knew what direction my life should take. I'm so thankful that God saw what I could not see.

There came a time when my grandmother went back to Florida to live with my uncle Wayne and his family. At that point in time, I was living by myself in the mobile home with just Fluffy and Ginger, the dog and cat that I had. It was the first time that I was living by myself since I had returned from Cincinnati, Ohio.

As a new Christian, I had to learn very early to depend upon God. There was a five-hundred-gallon gas tank sitting at the end of the mobile home, and the people who lived around me, or the people who were driving up and down the road, may have thought I was crazy, but that was okay because I was going out and standing at the gas tank, and I would raise the lid and look at the meter. I would pray and ask God to keep gas in the tank because I did not have money to put gas in the tank. One day, I looked at the meter, and it was sitting at 20 percent, so I talked to the lady at Litters, where we purchased our gas, and she told me that if the gauge was sitting at 20 percent, I only had a ten-day supply of gas. But as I kept praying, God was keeping gas in the tank because, you see, I had a gas hot water heater and a gas stove with which I did the cooking, and I did not get any money to put any gas in the tank until around October or the first part of November of 1987, but I never had one gas fume or no odor of gas.

That was the first time that, as a young Christian, I had put God to the test when I was asking for what I needed, and He was true and faithful to answer that need. That is when I began to understand that God knew everything and saw everything about my life.

A short time after I was saved, I went to visit some friends of mine, or people that I thought were friends of mine, Rick and Kathy Jones, who were two people that had also rented a house that was owned by my mother and father. It was the same house that my grandmother and I had lived in for a short time. The property where my mobile home was located was part of the property on which that house was located. When I went to visit them, the first thing they asked when I arrived was if I wanted a beer, and I politely said no, I did not. I then told them that I had gotten saved and given my heart to the Lord and I no longer wanted that to be a part of my life because, you see, several years before, on New Year's Eve, which happened to be Kathy's birthday, and they were still living in my mother and father's house, we decided we were going to play poker, but Kathy decided she wanted some cherry vodka for her birthday. So Rick and I drove to Chillicothe to buy some. As we were playing cards, Rick asked if I was going to play cards or drink. He was mixing the drinks in eight-ounce water glasses. When we had finished playing cards, I had gotten up from the table and was sitting on the arm of the chair. When I went to stand up, I realized that I was unstable and could not walk down the hill to go home, which, since our mobile home was not that far from the house, was on the same property. So I decided to lie down on the floor and go to sleep in the living room, and since it was my mother and father's house, I knew it would be okay. At one point, I was going to throw up, so I crawled on my hands and knees to the bathroom. I had my head in the toilet. About that time, Rick said he needed to go to the bathroom, and I told him he could not because I was already in there. So as far as I know, he threw up in the bedroom. After I threw up, I crawled back to the living room and went back to sleep until morning. But that was the last time I got drunk or drank anything that had to do with alcohol. But when I told them I was now a Christian and I did not want anything to do with any alcoholic beverages, they told me that I was too good to have anything to do with them. I told them that was not true, and for whatever reason, I have not spoken to them since.

As time went on, and I began to become more involved with the things that were going on at church, because my faith in God and love for Him was growing, I began to understand that He would be there for me when no one else was. There was another time when I was at home with Fluffy and Ginger, and I knew it was going to storm because you could hear thunder and lightning, and the electricity had gone off. Most of the windows in the mobile home were open, so even though it was dark and I could barely see, I had to get up to close the two windows in my bedroom. There was one window open in the hallway, and two windows open on the backside of the mobile home which had to be closed, and there was one window in the kitchen that was open. Before I prepared to close the windows, I sat on the side of my bed and began to pray, because I knew that if it started to rain before I got the windows closed, I would be getting water inside the mobile home. I got up and closed the windows. I closed the two windows in my bedroom; I didn't close the one in the hallway. Then I closed the two on the backside of the living room, and I closed the one in the kitchen at the end of the trailer, and once it was closed, I was standing in the middle of the kitchen floor, and it began to rain. But once again, that was a situation where I had asked God to let me get the windows closed before it started to rain.

I went back to my room and sat on the side of my bed. I realized that God had once again answered my prayer. As I sat there, I began to pray another prayer of thanks, and I told God that I was His and everything that I had was His, and if He wanted me to have it, He could take care of me and take care of it as well. As time went on, I also realized that there were many people who had been Christians for many years, that I had as examples of what God could do. I knew that if He could keep them, He could also keep me, and the only thing that I had to do was stay faithful and do as He asked me to do because if I do that, there is nothing that God will not do for me if I ask Him and truly need it. Because as the Bible says, ask and it shall be given to you, seek and you shall find, knock and it shall be opened unto you. I knew beyond the shadow of a doubt that God would keep His promises to His children.

As time went on, I made many new Christian friends, some of which were Joe and Norma Schageal and their sons, Mike, Rob, and Joe Jr.

The four of us spent a lot of time together doing many different things. At one point in time, I was voted in as third Elder and played the role of youth leader of the youth group. So when it came time for the youth rallies each month, Joe and Norma would go along. Joe would drive the van, and the two of them would also serve as chaperones.

There were several other people that I became acquainted with and good friends with at Pleasant Valley Plug Run Church. One of them was a lady whose name was Shirley Miller. She was a Sunday school teacher, and I still remember a remark she made one Sunday morning when she was teaching Sunday school, and she said that if we knew something about someone that would hurt someone if it came out, we would be better off not to say anything at all. The other thing that I remember about Shirley Miller that stands out in my memory to this day is one year when she and I were voted as delegates to counsel at Nipgen camp. That morning, Shirley picked me up at my home, and as we were driving to camp that morning, she told me that she had had a dream. In that dream, the two of us were at church at Plug Run, and in the dream, there were other people there as well. The two of us walked out of the church while the others remained there. As we got outside, she said the two of us began to rise up into the air, and then we were walking as though we were walking past a train station with people going here and there. And then, she said, all at once, I dropped my crutches and started running, and she told me later that she took that to mean that when I dropped my crutches, I must have been getting close to the gates of heaven. But then, she said, she woke up.

There was another friend of mine, and his name was Tim Uhrig. The two of us, from time to time, would go on visitation to people within the community, and he had been a member of the Uhrig Brothers quartet.

There was another special person who was attending Pleasant Valley Plug Run Church. She happened to be my grandmother's niece. Her name was Opal Grub. She was a wonderful Christian lady with a love for God and the community in which she lived. For many years, Opal did work in the community of Huntington Township. During the Christmas season, she usually had her son, Randy, dress up as Santa Claus when they would go to pass out gifts at Christmas. Opal's mother was a sister to my grandmother, Maxine. A lot of things went on during but one of the things that I remember fondly was when it was time for Nipgen camp meeting. The last Sunday of camp meeting would begin with services at our home church, but once that was over, a number of us would go to Opal's house on Valley Road to have a quick lunch before going on to Nipgen camp for an afternoon of gospel singing by groups that had been invited to sing that afternoon.

Another special time at church each year was our homecoming revival. For several years, our church always tried to get the Morgantown Trio as the singers and the Reverend Charlie Ragland as the evangelist. Not only did you get wonderful preaching, but when the Holy Spirit would begin moving and the Morgantown Trio were singing, Reverend Ragland would join right in and sing along with them, and then you would feel like the roof was going to come off of the top of the church because of the way the Holy Spirit would be moving in those services. The last Sunday of our homecoming revivals was very much like those of camp meetings in the fact that we would have dinner on the grounds and then have a Sunday afternoon with several groups invited to come and sing. Those were wonderful memories, and sometimes, with the way the world is today, I sometimes wish we could return to those days. Another of my memories from many years ago was one of a couple who lived on Mingo Road. There was a couple who lived up the road from the church; their names were Roberta and Lloyd Mendenhall. Lloyd's health was not very good, and he did not get out very much, but every once in a while, his wife Roberta would get him in the car, and they would go for a ride, but usually without fail, it would be on a night when we were having church services, and she would stop the car in front of the church. Somehow, someone would realize that they were sitting outside in the car, and most of the congregation would go stand outside the church and sing for them, which we all knew that they enjoyed very much, and the members of our church also enjoyed it.

There was also something that I began to do as my faith in God increased. I do not exactly remember whether it was something that I heard a visiting preacher preach about in a sermon or if it was something that I read about in the Bible, but there was a point in time when I began fasting. When I first started fasting, I was still living in my mobile home, and it was something that I very quickly realized must be taken very seriously. There came a point before most of the revivals I would begin fasting.

I remember after I first got saved, my mother gave me a set of cassette tapes that had the entire Bible on those tapes. So I would listen to cassette tapes and read my Bible along with it while listening. Then I began to pray for sanctification. While I was listening to the tapes, Reverend Don Pfeifer was on a tape I was listening to. It just so happened that year at Nipgen camp, Reverend Pfeifer and Reverend Donovan Humble were taking turns preaching at camp meetings. One of them would preach one night, and the other one would preach the next night. As I said, I had been praying for sanctification. I went to the altar at the camp meeting; I told God that night that I would do whatever He wanted me to do, I would go wherever He wanted me to go, and I would say whatever He wanted me to say. At that point, I was totally His, and He could use me any way He saw fit to do anything that He wanted me to do. When I was at the altar, I had a feeling hit me from the top of my head to the soles of my feet, and that had been almost thirty-two years ago, and what I received from God back then was as good today as it was at that time, for God has been and will be as faithful to me as He promised in His word that He would be to each of His children. There is one other thing that I remember about camp meeting that year, and it was one night when Reverend Don Pfeifer was preaching. That night, as Reverend Pfeifer began to preach, he did not preach from the pulpit. There was a small ledge in front of it that was probably no more than two and a half to three inches wide. When he began to preach, he was standing on that small ledge, and all of the time he was preaching, he was walking back and forth on that same ledge and never missed a step and never missed a word of his sermon. So that was another point when I realized that a person could do whatever God wanted them to do, no matter where they were and whatever position they were in.

There came a time in my life when I knew that it was up to God if I was supposed to have someone to spend my life with. So one night at church, I went to the altar, and I began to pray, and I asked the Lord that if He wanted me to have someone, it was up to Him to find the person that I was supposed to be with, for after having tried dating, I realized that I would not be able to choose the right person.

Shirley Miller happened to be one of several people who were at the altar when I prayed that prayer to God, and after having God answer so many of my prayers, I knew that if it was to happen, it would be in God's time and not mine.

There was one time when there were seven unsaved husbands of women who attended our church, so the church began to pray for each unsaved husband one day each week. One night, when I was praying at home before going to bed, I was praying for Joe Schaegel. That night, as I was praying for him, I told the Lord that if it took me getting up and going back to Joe for him to get saved, I would do it. Once I had finished praying for Joe, I began to pray for some of the kids I went to school with, and for some strange reason, I asked the Lord where Leona Hinty was. Little did I know that a question as simple as that would become the answer to one of my prayers. So it just goes to show that sometimes a very simple question can be an answer to a very important part of a person's life and future.

There came a time on a Sunday morning when Sunday school had ended, and they had taken the kids out to the trailer in which they had junior church. My mother helped out with junior church, so that Sunday morning, she was not present in the regular Sunday morning service. As the service continued, the first elder of our church was sitting up on the platform next to the pastor, Reverend Mosley, but you could feel the presence of the Holy Spirit. You knew that He was dealing with someone. First Elder Tim Uhrig came down off the platform and walked back and was talking to Joe. I could not hear what he was saying to him, but Joe kept saying no, no, no, no. Finally, Tim gave up and went back up and sat on the platform next to Reverend Mosley. At that point, God spoke to me and said, "Get up and go back to Joe as you had promised in your prayer." So without thinking, I got up and walked back to Joe, who was sitting approximately two or three pews behind the one that I was sitting in. When I got to the pew in front of him, I sat down and began to talk to him. As I was talking to him, I told him he needed to go to the altar and get saved. Joe told me later, and I do not know if it was when I was walking back to him or when I sat down to talk to him, that he had fire under his feet, and he knew that he had to move and go to the altar. When he got up to go to the altar, I was going to go up with him, but that was when I realized that I did not have my crutches with me, for they were still lying underneath the pew in front of the one that I had been sitting in. So when the Lord told me to get up and go back to him, I got up and went without my crutches. Norma, Joe's wife, told me later that I walked better that day without my crutches than I did when I used them. As we all got to the altar and Joe began to pray, he was also pounding on the altar, and it felt that as God was saving and forgiving Joe, I felt that whatever Joe was getting was going through me as well because I had honored my prayer to God where Joe was concerned, and I think God was rewarding me because I had done so. I had put God to the test many times before, but this time, He gave me the power and the strength to do what I had promised Him I would do.

Chapter 9

There came a time, as I remember, it was after Thanksgiving but within about a week of Christmas, when my mother had received a telephone call from my uncle Wayne in Florida. During that call, my mother was told that my grandmother had cancer of the colon, and he said that she was not doing very well. If we wanted to see her, we needed to come to Florida as soon as possible. So I then asked Mike, Joe Jr., and Rob to stay at my house and take care of Fluffy and Ginger, and make sure nothing happened while I was gone to Florida. My mother had given me a microwave as a present for Christmas, and since I got it before we left, the boys decided to try to use it to cook hot dogs, and they told me later that the hot dogs exploded. As I remember, I believe we left on a Friday night to go to Florida. We had been driving for quite a while, we had driven out of Ohio, through Kentucky, and were somewhere in the state of Tennessee. I remember it must have been somewhere that you needed to stop because I remember that we stopped at a gas station to fill up with gas, and there was a sign there that said if you did not get gas there, you had to go 250 miles before you reached the next gas station going up a mountain. I do not know whether we had gone any further than the 250 miles that the previous sign had said or not, but I do remember that we finally stopped at a gas station, and I think we all went to the restroom, but my parents asked the attendant if we would be allowed to park at the side of the parking lot for the night.

The next morning when I woke up, my father was driving through Atlanta, Georgia, at 8:00 a.m. There were a couple of things that were different about Atlanta: one was that there were six lanes of traffic on each side of the highway, and the other was that the speed limit was eighty miles an hour, and everyone was headed to work at that time of the morning, and if you did not keep up with the traffic, you might get run over.

When we finally got to Florida, the first place we went was to see my grandmother, and she was in a Receiving Hospital in Macclenny, Florida. When we got there and we walked into her room, someone got me a chair, and as I was sitting there, realizing that my grandmother did not know that I was there and the fact that she was strapped down in the bed.

As I was sitting by her, she was looking straight at me, and yet she did not know that I was right there, and that was when I started to cry. At that point, I asked God because I knew I could not handle it by myself, and He gave me a peace that I was able to handle everything else that happened from that point on.

When we left the hospital that night, I stayed in my uncle Wayne's trailer because it was easier to get into than the one my grandmother had. That evening while we were sitting in his trailer, my uncle accused me and said that I had prayed to God for my grandmother to die. It was then that I had told him that that was not the prayer that I had prayed at all. I told him that I had asked God to do whatever it took for my grandmother to be saved, not to let her die. After we had finished the discussion, we both went to bed.

The next morning when we got up, we were going to take her to a hospital in Jacksonville, Florida, so all of us followed the ambulance in which she was riding. When we had gotten to the hospital where she had been the night before, when we walked in that morning, she knew my mother and father, and as I was walking down the hall, I heard her tell my mother, "Here comes Pokie," which was my nickname. But by the time we had gotten to Jacksonville, it was just like it had been the night before, and she did not recognize any of us. At that point, there were times when I would be sitting in her room with her when she said she could see things out of her window. One time, she even told me that she saw pink elephants. That was because her room was on the seventh floor of the hospital, and every time I would take a break, and since I did not know where the chapel was in the hospital because it was so big, I would walk around the corner to a sitting area that had a restroom, and I would go in the restroom, go into one of the stalls, shut the door, and pray and ask God to help me, and I had to do that on several different occasions.

One afternoon, as my uncle Wayne, my father, and I were sitting in the common area, my father said that he wished he had never said or done what had occurred that caused my grandmother to go back to Florida. Another thing that occurred while the three of us were sitting there was that my father had told me that he was proud of me, that I had turned out to be a very good person, and that I had accomplished a lot. I remember on Christmas Day, I was sitting in my uncle's trailer, and it was eighty degrees and sunshine on Christmas day with no snow, and I thought to myself, *This is not Christmas.* Several days later, they put my grandmother in a step-down unit, but my mother, father, and I decided that we could come home back to Chillicothe, which we did.

Once we returned home, my father took me back up to my house. When we got there, my father and I were standing in the kitchen, and the two of us were talking. He told me that he was proud of me and that I had turned out to be a good person. When he told me he was proud of me, he then said all that he ever wanted me to do was to be able to stand on my own two feet, make a decision, and not be afraid to make it. I thanked him for what he had said, and I told him that it was all right because I knew that he had done the best he could do when I was growing up. He did not know how to deal with someone in a situation like the one I was in as far as my handicap was concerned, but I told him I knew that he had done the best that he could do under the circumstances. Then things kind of returned to normal once we had returned home, and for the most part, the things that went on revolved around the things that happened in church.

When my grandmother had gone to Florida, she had wanted or needed money, I think it was to buy the mobile home that she had down there on my uncle's property. So my mother went to the credit union and set up a loan through them for me to buy her half of the mobile home that we had when we had lived together. Over time, I paid back the loan at the credit union, so the mobile home was legally mine.

One day, my mother came up to my house to talk to me, and the question she asked me was whether or not I would let my grandmother come back and live with me since the mobile home was mine. Of course, there was no doubt as to what my answer would be. Of course, I said yes. From what I gathered, my grandmother had told my uncle Wayne that if she was going to die, she wanted to go home to die, and she also told him, "Steve knows how to pray," which was probably a shock to him after he had accused me of asking God to let her die. I guess it just goes to show how, when we as Christians talk to God, God knows what we say when we ask or pray for something, but it is strange how people can jump to other conclusions without even knowing what was said between the person praying and God Himself.

So my mother and father prepared to make another trip to Florida to pick up my grandmother and bring her back to Ohio. I imagine the trip back to Florida only took one day to get there, and once they had picked up my grandmother, my mother talked to the doctors, and they told her that when she got my grandmother back to Ohio, to get her to the hospital and run the test again for cancer. But a strange thing happened as they prepared for the trip back home. As they started home, it began to snow, and the people down south were not used to a lot of snow, besides the fact that they do not have a lot of snow removal equipment. My father told me that they had to stop overnight at a hotel or motel because the roads were so bad, they could not travel. The next morning, he said he got behind a snowplow on the highway and stayed behind it most of the way. I think by the time they got a little further north, maybe to Tennessee or Kentucky, the weather conditions had improved. When they finally got home, one of my parents came up to my house to pick me up so I could go down to their house to see my grandmother. While I was down there that evening, my mother and I had prayer with my grandmother before I went back to my house.

My mother had done as the doctor in Florida had told her. She took my grandmother to Riverside Hospital in Columbus, where they ran the tests for colon cancer, and it was present. She was then scheduled for surgery. Apparently, they had taken her down to the operating room. The next thing my grandmother knew when she came to herself, the doctors were marching around her bed. They told her she was a miracle because when they went to do her surgery, the cancer was gone.

My grandmother finally came back to live with me in our mobile home, and things returned to normal for both of us, but most of the things that happened still revolved around church and the things that were going on there. There was a time when we were getting ready for a revival, and there had been a lady who played the piano at church on a previous occasion. Her name was Donna Baker. In one of our board meetings, when we were talking about and planning for future revivals and we were trying to schedule a singer and a preacher for a youth revival, and at that time, I was the youth leader, so I was on the board. It was decided to ask Donna Baker if she would sing for our youth revival, and Reverend Tim Case was to be the evangelist for that revival.

Reverend Mosley then contacted Donna Baker, and she told Reverend Mosley that she would come for six hundred dollars for the week. So during a Sunday service, Reverend Mosley asked for pledges to help pay for the cost of Donna for the revival. Since the revival was later in the year, that gave members of the congregation time to pay their pledges. Even though I was on a fixed income, I pledged twenty-five dollars, but little did I know how the Lord would bless me for doing so.

One day, Tim Uhrig came to see me at home, which was a surprise. I was sitting in my room watching television when Tim walked in, and he told me that he had been told by someone else to give me something. Then he proceeded to hand me fifty dollars, which was double the amount of my pledge that I had made to help pay the cost of Donna Baker coming for the youth revival. Tim then proceeded to tell me that he had gone to his insurance agent to pay his insurance. He must have told the insurance agent about the pledge that I had made. His insurance agent, whose names were David and Carolyn Lee of Adena Insurance in Frankfort, Ohio, told Tim that he had overpaid on his insurance. Tim went on to tell me that David Lee had told him to give me the fifty dollars that he had overpaid on his insurance. So once again, that was another time when God had blessed something that I had done because that was something that God led me to do. That was similar to something that had happened to my mother one time at church. When they were taking up an offering, my mother had two dollars. She put the two dollars, and later she looked in her purse or whatever she was carrying her money in that time, and there was still two dollars. My mother went and asked if she had put two dollars in the offering the first time, and the person told her she had. This shows an occasion where she had done as God had asked, and even though there was no doubt that she had put the two dollars in the offering, there was still two dollars in her purse.

When the youth revival came around, as the youth leader of our church, it was my responsibility to lead the service.

As I was sitting on the platform as the service began that night, we were having prayer, and I was kneeling while I was praying. Donna Baker began to play a song on the piano, and I felt the Holy Spirit leading me to go back and talk to someone, to try the spirit to make sure what I was supposed to do and to make sure it was what God wanted me to do. While I was praying, I asked God to give me a sign by letting Donna play that song again, which she did when He answered as I asked. I then walked off the platform.

My cousin Michelle Miller was sitting in the back of the church, and at the time, I thought she might have been the only unsaved person in the church that night. Michelle told me that when I stepped off the platform, she knew that I was coming back to her. She also said she wanted to hide. Fortunately, Michelle gave her heart to the Lord that night. The Holy Spirit was moving very strongly in that service, but little did any of us know at the time that the Holy Spirit was at several other places as well.

Later that evening, when we got home, we received several phone calls. One call was from Shirley Miller, letting us know that her husband, Frank, had been sitting on his front porch with a beer in his hand, but all at once, he threw away the beer into the middle of the yard, and he never drank another one. So not only was the Holy Spirit at church that night, he was also at Frank and Shirley Miller's home on Poplar Ridge Road. Frank Miller also happened to be the father-in-law of my cousin Michelle. We got another phone call that Shep Penrod, who lived in Knockemstiff, had also been saved at his home. He was eighty-nine years old at the time he was saved. So that night was living proof that, as the Bible says, God and the Holy Spirit can be omnipresent, which means they can be anywhere and everywhere all the time.

A short time later, things began to change in a way that I never expected. My niece, Christina, had invited her grandmother and grandfather, Dana and Edna Pritchard, out to our church at Pleasant Valley Plug Run. After coming for several weeks, Edna invited her brother and sister-in-law to come as well. At that time, I did not realize who they were, but to my surprise, Edna's sister-in-law was going home and telling her daughter, a person that she loved to hear testify. The only thing her mother knew was the young man's first name was Steve. Her daughter asked her if she thought it could be Steve Penrod, and her mother told her that she did not know because the pastor only used first names.

Sometime later, the church was having a revival. Her mother invited her to go with them one night, which the young lady did. When they arrived at the church and she walked in, she recognized a lady that she remembered from many years ago, and it happened to be my mother, Geraldine. She asked her if I was there, and my mother told her that I was there, sitting in the second row from the front. My mother asked her if she wanted to walk up and say hello, and she said no because she was at the back. So my mother told her that she would walk up with her to where I was sitting. When they walked up there, the young lady looked at me and said, "Do you know who I am?" and I said, "No, I do not." When she told me who she was, I was totally shocked because she did not look like she had looked years before, but at the same time, the first thing that popped into my mind was the prayer I had prayed when I asked the Lord where she was. Her name was Leona Hinty, and the two of us had gone to school together at Mount Logan, and we had both been in the class of Mrs. Lucille Carter. Leona told me later that I kept making her nervous because I kept turning around and looking at her, but the thing that she did not realize was that I knew God answered my prayer when I had asked Him where she was, and little did either one of us know that she was the answer to another prayer that I had prayed when I went to the altar at church.

Chapter 10

As I said at the end of the last chapter, when Leona came to the revival that night, she did not know that she was an answer to a prayer, and at that time, I did not know that she had prayed a similar prayer, asking God to find someone for her to spend the rest of her life with. The fact that we did not like each other when we went to school together even makes this story sound a little strange. But once she came to church, she kept coming, as both of us later discovered God's plan for us would be nothing like what we thought it would be. As time went on, I was given her phone number, and we began to talk to each other on the telephone. I do not recall how long it was, but there came a point in time when I told her that I was falling in love with her. Of course, she told me I was crazy because she did not want anything to do with me. But I guess that also goes to show that God is in control of everything that happens to each of us, even though we may not realize it at the time. But everything that happens to each of His children happens in God's time, and His timing is always perfect.

God's vision for His people is greater and goes deeper than any of us can ever see because we cannot see what God sees; we cannot know what God knows. But God knows the reason behind everything that happens to everyone, those who are saved and those who are not saved, for the Bible says that God is no respecter of persons, and God's wish is that each of us would be saved so that we may have a personal relationship with Him.

God puts people in our lives to help show us and let us know the direction in which we should go because each of our lives has its own direction and purpose. When Leona started coming to Pleasant Valley Plug Run, I felt like God was letting me know that she was the answer to the prayer I had prayed when I told God it was up to Him if I was to have a mate. In the beginning, I don't think she understood what was happening because when I told her I was falling in love with her, she told me I was crazy, and she did not want anything to do with me. But God knew better than both of us what was supposed to happen.

As time went on, I began to realize what God was doing, and when I felt as though I knew that Leona and I were meant to be together, when I would pray, I would ask the Lord different things about the situation. I would ask Him things like if we were meant to be together, then I was going to have to buy a car, and since I didn't have any money, I didn't know how that was going to happen. But as I began to realize, this time waiting on God had everything under control. When Leona and I would talk on the phone, when we may not be talking about anything in particular, but if it was late at night, she would start getting the giggles, and when she started getting the giggles, she would make me laugh. There was one night when I was talking to her, when it started to happen, and then I started to laugh, and I was laughing so hard, I ended up falling off of my bed onto the floor, and I think she heard me because she asked me what I was doing, and I said, "It's all your fault because I'm on the floor."

When we finally decided to sit together at church, she still would not sit up front with me, so I began to sit about midway back in the church because that is where she wanted to sit. It got to the point that everyone at church was asking if I had backslid because I wasn't sitting in the front anymore, where I usually sat.

Everything that happened between the two of us always seemed to happen at church. There was one night in particular when Shirley Miller was talking to Leona, and she told her that she was an answer to a prayer. Leona did not understand what Shirley was talking about. I understood what she was talking about, and it was like a light bulb went off in my head because I knew that the two of us were supposed to be together.

I remember going home one night, and as I was praying before going to bed, I told God that if we were supposed to be together, there were many things that would have to be worked out. But little did I know, God was one step ahead of me with everything that I was praying about because, as I said, I did not have any money to buy a car. The only thing I owned was the satellite dish, which, in God's plan, turned into an automobile, even though it was one that Leona could not drive because it had a standard transmission. At that point, I put an ad in the advertiser, trying to sell my satellite dish. Once I put the ad in, I had one gentleman call me and ask me how much I wanted for my satellite dish, and I told him I didn't know, but I needed enough money to buy a car because I was getting married. Thankfully, he told me he had a car that he would trade me straight up for my satellite dish. So he brought the car out to my house and let me look at it to see if I liked it. After I looked at it, the two of us made a deal, so then I had a car. God had taken care of one problem.

Another night I was praying, I told the Lord that if Leona and I were to get married, she would have to get her driver's license since I did not drive. The Lord must have been paying very close attention to what I prayed because the very next morning, Leona called me, and before I could say anything, she told me she was going to get her driver's license. That was when I realized that God was working on both ends to help Leona and me.

We did a lot of different things at Pleasant Valley Plug Run Church. On one occasion, we were having a bean dinner at the church. The gentleman who was cooking the beans was using a three-legged iron kettle and a boat oar to stir them. After Leona and I had finished eating, the two of us decided to walk back and visit Sandy Hines, who was a friend of ours who lived in a trailer behind the church. As we were walking back through there, I looked at Leona and said, "I am more comfortable with you than anybody I've ever been with," and then I was shaking my head, wondering why I had said that.

We got back to Sandy's and visited for a while, but what Leona and I didn't realize until later was that there was a group of ladies watching the two of us. What we did not know was that they were discussing the two of us between themselves. We later discovered that they had been talking to each other and saying it would be nice if the Lord would work something out between the two of us, which is exactly what God was doing, but they did not know that at the time. At one point, apparently, my mother walked up to where they were standing, and they did not know what to say because they did not know how she would react. It seemed like everything that happened between the two of us took place at church, which was a sign to us that God meant for us to be together.

When Leona and I went on our first date, we double-dated with Mike and Kelly, a friend of Leona's. Since it was my first date with Leona and Mike's first date with Kelly, Mike had told me that he could get a dozen roses for each of them for nineteen dollars apiece. So I told him to get a dozen for Leona, and he got a dozen for Kelly. At that point, Leona did not yet have her driver's license, even though we had a car, so Mike drove his mother's car that night. When Mike and I arrived to pick up Kelly and Leona, I gave Leona the roses I had gotten for her, and Mike did the same with the roses he got for Kelly. Then we went out on a date. The four of us went to a gospel concert at Huntington Hall on US 23 South, close to Massieville. There were four groups at the concert that night; the two headline groups were the Perry Sisters and the Singing Cooks. When we first arrived, I was talking to a gentleman who was making videotapes of the concert. He said that anyone who wanted one could have a copy for twenty dollars, but he said he was not allowed to put the Perry Sisters on the video. However, I decided that I wanted one anyway, so I paid him twenty dollars in advance to get one when they were finished. The concert was very nice, with a lot of wonderful singing. During intermission, Leona and I decided to get up and walk around a little bit. As we were walking around, I went by a table set up by the Singing Cooks. As I was talking to the gentleman at the table, I told him that I would like to have something that they had at the table, and I asked him what the price was for whatever I was looking at. He told me the price was twenty dollars, and I said I would like to have it, but I didn't have that much money because I was going out to dinner with my girlfriend after the concert. I told him I only had ten dollars to spare. He told me ten dollars was enough because, he said, ten dollars would buy him a hamburger at McDonald's, at the drive-through. But what I did not know at the time was that the gentleman who was making the videotapes of the concert decided to put the Perry Sisters on the video anyway, even though he was not supposed to do so. What I did not realize at the time was that Leona and I ended up being in the video.

After the concert, Mike, Kelly, Leona, and I went out to dinner at Jr. Valentine's. We enjoyed the meal, but after we had finished eating, we were preparing to take the girls home. When we got to the girls' houses, my car was parked across the street in the Kerr's Distributing parking lot, which was across from their houses. All of a sudden, Leona started laughing, and then she said, "I can't go home yet." The four of us took off again on another ride.

As we were driving down East Main Street, when we stopped at the lights, Kelly said they looked like Christmas lights because they were red and green, and all of us were having a good time laughing at each other and acting silly. We ended up going out Blacksmith Hill and ended up going to Ross Lake. When we got there, Mike parked the car in the parking lot. Mike and Kelly decided to take a walk, which meant that Leona and I were in the back seat of the car by ourselves. The strange thing was that every time Leona would look at me, she would start laughing. I never knew why she had such a strange reaction. When Mike and Kelly returned to the car, they asked if we had done anything, and I said no because every time she looked at me, she started laughing. At that point, we were finally able to take the girls home. It must have been about 2:30 a.m., and by the time Mike had dropped me off at my house, it was around 3:00 a.m., and Mike still had to drive home. He did not get home until approximately 3:30 a.m., and his mother was fit to be tied.

There's something else that I must mention here that was really very funny. One night, when I was talking to Leona on the phone, her future son, Chris, told his mother that we should hurry up and get married so we did not run up the electric bill. So as time went on, God continued to move things in the direction they needed to go. As I said before, most of the things happened at church. One night during a revival, the service was over, with the exception of the altar call. Leona's friend, Kelly, went to the altar that night, but Leona and

I were already outside the church, standing beside her father's car, talking. I have always said that God kept everything simple so that I wouldn't mess it up. While standing by the car, I looked at Leona and said, "Do you want to?" and she said, "I do if you do," and that is exactly what I said to her, and she knew exactly what I meant when I said it, for that was how I asked her to marry me. When she said yes, I said, "Let's wait before we tell anyone," and she said, Okay."

So as time went on, we didn't tell anyone that we had decided we were getting married. But then one night, everything changed when Leona called and my grandmother answered the phone. Or when she answered the phone, my grandmother said, "I think it's your future wife on the phone." And after she had brought me the phone, when I picked it up, Leona asked me if I had told her anything, and I said "No, I had not," but I then told Leona I would tell her when I got off the phone with her, which was exactly what I did. When I got off the phone with Leona, I told my grandmother to come into my room and that I needed to talk to her.

When my grandmother came into my room, I told her that Leona and I were going to get married. That is when she told me she wasn't surprised, but then she said, "I don't know what your mother is going to say," to which I responded, "It doesn't matter what she says."

Then there came a Sunday morning when Joe Schageal Jr. was getting married. By that time, I had Leona sitting back in my normal spot, so I told her we might as well stay and watch what we were going to have to go through. Once their ceremony had finished, I looked at Leona and said, "Do you want to go ahead and tell them?"

Then she said, "Go ahead."

As I looked at Reverend Mosley, who was still standing behind the pulpit, I said, "There is going to be another wedding down somewhere," to which he replied, "The whole church has been praying that the Lord would work something out between the two of you." So at that point, we realized that everything that had happened had been a part of God's plan all along.

After most people knew that Leona and I were going to get married, there were a lot of decisions to be made and details that needed to be worked out, so in some ways, it was a very busy time but also a very joyous time for everyone involved. But then there was also a funeral on the Penrod side of the family.

My grandmother and I were headed to the funeral home in Bainbridge for the viewing. As I remember, my grandmother told me that I should not say anything about the fact that I was getting married. She felt that the funeral home was not the place to talk about my wedding.

While we were there, I ran into a lot of my cousins, and as we got to talking, they asked what I was up to. As we began talking, I told them that I was getting married, but I also told them that my grandmother had told me not to say anything while we were at the funeral home. Then they asked me why, and I said I did not know, but they all told me that they wanted to come to my wedding, which I appreciated very much. And I told them it was sad that the only time we ever got together was when someone died because it had been fifteen or twenty years since we had had a family reunion. We set our original wedding date for June 2, 1990.

When Leona told me that she was going to get her driver's license, I told her I would help pay for half of her driver's training, which I did. We split the cost, so we each paid 150 dollars. When she got her permit, he would help out while she was practicing her driving. By that time, my mother had traded in the 1986 Yugo, which had a standard transmission, for a 1980 Pontiac that had an automatic transmission. So one day, Mike stopped at my house, left his car at my house, and drove the Pontiac to town. We then went to Leona's house and picked her up along with my future son, Chris, and her best friend, Kelly, and the four of us took off so Leona could practice her driving. When we were leaving, she asked me where I wanted to go. I told her she could go anywhere she wanted to because if we needed gas, I had money to put more gas in the car, so it didn't matter where we went. As things worked out, we ended up going back out to my house. We then went down Denver Road and happened to stop at Clyde and Donna McQuay's house. While we were there, we told them we were getting married. After that, we drove back to town and headed out to Charleston Pike. We ended up down in Tar

Hollow, which had a lot of old, bumpy, winding, narrow roads. I figured that if she could drive on those roads, she could drive anywhere, and I was absolutely correct. The funny thing about that day, though, was that Mike, Chris, and I were in the backseat, and Leona and Kelly were in the front seat, and just like on our first date with the traffic lights that Kelly said were Christmas lights, Kelly decided to take off her shoes, and she had her feet sticking out the window and had her socks fastened to the radio antenna of my car. As I said, Mike, Chris, and I were in the backseat, and Chris was chewing bubble gum, and all at once, he lost it, so the three of us in the backseat were trying to find Chris's bubblegum. Chris had to get a new piece of gum because, at first, we couldn't find the old one, and then we realized he was sitting on it, but there was not enough room back there to make sure where it was all of the time. So that was a good day in a lot of ways, but by the time we got back to Leona's house, I had made up my mind to let her go ahead and keep the car. So I told Kelly that if they would follow us out to my house, I would let Leona bring the car back. That way, she could use it when she took her driver's test, but in the long run, she decided to use the car from Neff's training school.

Shortly thereafter, she took her driver's test, passed it, and had her license, so that was another thing over the list of things that we had to do.

When Leona and I first talked about getting married, we said we wanted a small wedding. But as I've said all through this book, the Lord had other ideas. We had to make out the guest list and send out invitations. Leona had to choose her bridesmaid and maid of honor, and I had to choose my best man.

Michelle Miller, my cousin, was the bridesmaid. Kelly Wilson was Leona's maid of honor. My niece Christina was the flower girl, and our son, Chris was the ring bearer. Opal Grub was asked to make our wedding cake. So the plans were coming together, and we were going to have our reception in Doodle's garage, which he said he had originally built to be a carryout, but God turned it into a location where we could have all of our church dinners and that sort of thing.

The biggest thing I had to do was go to Overbrook Park Apartments on Anderson Station Road and apply for an apartment. When I first went out there and told them I was getting married, they told me I couldn't rent the apartment because I wasn't married already, and they also said that there was a six-month waiting list. And by the time I went out there to talk to them, there were less than six months before our original wedding date, so I didn't know what to do. However, as every other time before, God intervened because I got a phone call sometime in February of 1990, stating that I had an apartment, but I had to move quickly. I did not have any furniture, but my mother had some furniture that she wasn't using. I had one television set and a kitchen table and chairs from someone. I don't know if it was my mother's or not. Of course, that meant that we were going to have to move up the wedding date. The problem was the invitations had already been sent out.

My mother had told me she would take Leona shopping to find a wedding dress. So one day, the two of them took off and went to JC Penney Outlet in Columbus, Ohio, to see if they could find anything that Leona liked. Unfortunately, they did not, so my mother told Leona that they would check a couple of other places in Chillicothe. But before they left Columbus, they went out to lunch. Then when they got back to Chillicothe, they stopped at JoAnn Fabrics. Since they were unable to find anything, my mother told Leona that she would make her wedding dress, which she did.

There is one thing that I was not aware of that happened before the wedding. I did not realize that Leona had been taken to the emergency room on Thursday, and the ER doctor wanted to put her in the hospital. She had been diagnosed with an upper respiratory infection and a virus infection, but when the doctor wanted to admit her, she said, "You can't. I'm getting married on Sunday." So he told her to go get married and then go home and go to bed. So the wedding rehearsal was on Friday, the Twenty-Third, and the rehearsal went off without a hitch.

Mike came and stayed with me at the apartment on Saturday night before the wedding. We were scheduled to get married at three on Sunday afternoon. When we left for church that day, I was already dressed for the wedding, so I hung around with Mike until three in the afternoon when it was almost time for the wedding. The other strange thing about the wedding was the fact that Leona and I had said we wanted a small wedding when we first talked about getting married, but on that occasion, there were approximately 200 to 250 people at our wedding: family from both sides, members of the church, and other friends. As Mike and I were sitting in the other room waiting for the ceremony to start, they began to have to put people in with us. So there was Reverend Mosley, Mike, myself, and some of the Cox kids.

When it came time for us to walk out and stand and wait for Leona to come down the aisle, as I walked out, I looked at Leona's father, and he didn't say anything but gave me a strange look. As I looked around, the church was filled to capacity, and there were people standing against the back wall by the doors. Leona had asked her father to give her away, but he said he could not give his little girl away. Leona then asked her brother Robert if he would give her away. Not only did he not give her away, but he did not even show up for the wedding. So Leona's uncle Perry Gaines Jr. gave her away. Leona's aunt Peggy, who happened to be blind, sang a song, and then Keith Dearth, the church pianist, played the "Wedding March" as Leona and her uncle were walking down the aisle. I realized that God had answered the prayer that both of us had prayed when we told the Lord that if we were to have someone to spend our life with, it was up to God to find the person that we were meant to spend our life with, and that is exactly what He did.

As the ceremony began, Reverend Mosley said that marriage was something not to be entered into lightly or unadvisedly. Then he said, "If anyone could show just cause why these two should not be joined, let them speak now or forever hold their peace." Then Reverend Mosley asked, "Who gives this woman to this man?"

Then Leona's father said, "Her mother and I do."

Reverend Mosley then asked who had the rings. Our son, Chris, was the ring bearer. Leona's ring was taken off the pillow and handed to me, and then Reverend Mosley said, "Steven, repeat after me, 'With this ring, I thee wed. I, Steven, take thee, Leona, to be my lawful wedded wife, forsaking all others, keep thee only unto her, for better or worse, for richer or poorer, in sickness and in health, until death do us part.'"

Then Reverend Mosley was trying to get my ring off the pillow, but for some reason, he could not untie the knot. Finally, when he had the ring, he handed it to Leona and said, "Repeat after me, 'With this ring, I thee wed. I, Leona, take thee, Steven, to be my lawful wedded husband, forsaking all others, keep thee only unto him, for better or worse, for richer or poorer, in sickness and in health, until death do us part.'"

There was one thing that happened during Leona's part of the ceremony. When it came time for Leona to do her vows, somehow I knew that she was going to mess up. So I was looking down at the floor to keep from laughing in case she messed up her vows, which, as luck would have it, she did. But as the ceremony ended, Reverend Mosley said a prayer, and then he said, "I am glad to introduce to you, Mr. and Mrs. Steven Penrod. What God has joined together, let no man put asunder."

At that point, Leona and I walked down the aisle, and we were standing outside the church to greet all of our guests as they exited the church following the ceremony. The members of the wedding party remained so that pictures could be taken. We had pictures taken with both sets of parents, all of the grandparents, the bridesmaid and maid of honor, the best man, including the ring bearer and flower girl.

By late that afternoon, the weather had improved, and the sun came out. We then went to the reception, which was also well-attended. When we entered the reception, once again, we were introduced as Mr. and Mrs. Steven Penrod.

Leona and I cut our wedding cake before we were seated at the head table, and in the process, Leona decided to get cake all over my face. Then I took off her garter. When I threw it, Mike, my best man, was the one who caught it. Then, as Leona prepared to throw her bouquet, we had to tell the kids that they could not try to catch it, only adults could catch it. When Leona threw it, my grandmother Maxine was the one who caught it. I should have asked my grandmother if she was looking to get married since I would no longer be around.

My cousin Michelle was helping to handle the opening of our wedding gifts. Of course, Leona and I were not aware that the first gift that she gave Leona to open happened to be in a Tampax box. When she opened it, it had lingerie with three holes cut in the appropriate places. A friend of ours, Ronnie Posey, asked Leona to hold it up a second time because he said he did not get a good look at it the first time. As we continued to open our gifts, some were cards with money in them. I told Leona to give me the money, and she could have everything else. As time went on and we continued to visit with our guests, it started getting later, and both of us were ready to go home. What Leona and I did not realize is that Mike and Michelle had taken off and left the reception, and Reverend Mosley had said that he and Mike had forgotten to sign our marriage license. So even though the ceremony had taken place, we were not legally married until the marriage certificate was signed, so we had to wait for Mike to return, which he eventually did.

Once Mike and Michelle returned, our marriage license was signed, and we were preparing to leave, someone asked me if I was coming to church that night, and I said, "I don't think so."

Then someone said, "I know what you'll be doing." We were riding in the car of Leona's father on the way home. We decided to stop at the store to pick up a few things we needed. Leona and I both went into the grocery store; I was still in my suit, and she was still in her wedding dress. We walked around the store picking up the things we needed, and we got a few things for our son, Chris. As we went through the checkout, the cashier asked if we had just gotten married, and we said yes because the Just Married sign was still on the back of the car of Leona's father.

Chapter 11

When we got home after the reception and stopping at the grocery store, Leona's mother and father pulled into our parking space by our apartment. At that time, we lived in a handicapped apartment all the way up to the top of the hill. When we pulled in, we realized that there was toilet paper all over the bushes and wrapped around the railing leading up to our front door. As we unloaded the things we had bought at the store, the things were taken and set by the front door. When we all got up to the door, Leona went to stick the key in the door and realized that there was Vaseline all over the doorknob. Even after she put the key in, she tried to open the door and could not turn the knob because it was slick, and she could not turn it. So then we had to find something to wipe the knob off with before we could open the door to go into the apartment.

By the time we got home, it was dark, so we had to try to turn the lights on when we went in the door, but we realized that there was also Vaseline on the light switches. As we checked around the rest of the apartment, there was a pair of women's panties in the refrigerator and a bra in the freezer. They had also put Vaseline on the toilet seat. Since we had a four-poster bed, when we checked the bedroom, we found toilet paper tied on all four corners of the bedposts, and there was rice in the bed. Leona still wasn't feeling well, so she dumped the rice out of the bed sheets, and then I think we all got a bite to eat. Since Leona wasn't feeling well and Chris had school the next day, they both went on to bed, but I had to stay up because Reverend Mosley was supposed to bring our wedding gift to us after church that night, and they were loaded in the back of his pickup truck. So we sat and watched television and waited for him to show up. I don't know whether they had loaded the gifts on the truck before church or not because, by the time he got to the apartment, it was about eight thirty or nine o'clock. Once he got there and unloaded the gifts, the gifts were left in the living room until the next morning. So I was finally able to lock the door and go to bed.

When I finally got in bed, I thought Leona was already asleep because she was sick, so I didn't say anything. Then all at once, she said, "Are we going to do anything or not?" and I said, "I thought you were asleep."

The next morning, we had to get up at about seven thirty to take Chris to school at Tiffin. That was where he had been going to school before we had gotten married, and because it was late in the school year, we decided not to make Chris change schools until the following fall.

The next few days, life continued to return to normal, even though everything was a new beginning for all three of us.

When Wednesday night came around, Leona was still not feeling well, so I decided to go to church with Robin Castle, who lived in the apartment next to ours at Overbrook Park Apartments. It was on a Wednesday evening, and when I left, everything seemed fine, except Leona was still getting over what she had had when she went to the emergency room before we got married. We had a good service that night at church. When the service was over, Robin and I returned home. When the two of us got back to the apartment, Robin's husband, Tracy, came out and told us that Leona had an accident. Our son, Chris, had stayed at home with his mother, and he had to call his grandparents to take his mother to the emergency room. When I was finally able to get into the apartment, there seemed to be blood everywhere, and I wondered what had happened. A little while later, Leona's parents returned with her and Chris from the emergency room at the hospital. Leona needed three stitches to close the wound on her hand, which went clear to the bone. I was thankful that she was alright. Then I told Leona, "I don't know if it's safe to leave you by yourself or not."

We would have to get up at about seven thirty in the morning to get ready to take Chris to school at Tiffin, and Leona and

I would return home and try to get whatever needed to be done as we continued to settle into our new life together. There was a Laundromat down at the bottom of the hill by the office. There were four washers and four dryers, which could be used by everyone who lived in the complex. Because there were only four washers and four dryers for everyone who lived there, and if they were being used, you would have to wait your turn. So Leona and I started going out to my grandmother's to do our laundry. She had an old wringer washer, and you rinsed your clothes in a washtub. But whenever we needed to do laundry, we would drop Chris off at school and then go out to do our laundry while he was in school that day. The other thing about doing our laundry out there was that we were able to hang our clothes on the line. So we would finish the laundry, hang the clothes on the line to dry, and then drive back to Chillicothe to pick up Chris after school. And then when we felt like the laundry was dry, we would go back out and pick it up. Besides, doing our laundry that way was free.

We made several new friends when we moved into Overbrook Park. There were some whom Leona had known before we got married, but there were some whom we did not know. As I said before, Robin Castle lived in the apartment next to ours. She lived in apartment 130, and we lived in apartment 131. Robin also attended Pleasant Valley Plug Run Church. Robin's mother was the Sunday school superintendent; her name was Ellen Posey. Robin had a little girl, her name was Amanda, and she loved to come to our house, especially when Leona was making homemade french fries because Amanda said that Leona's french fries were better than McDonald's french fries.

We had other friends that we met while we were living there. Two of them were Larry and Becky Young. They had two boys. Larry and Becky's two boys used to play with our son, Chris. Some of our other friends were Wayne Thomas and Tonya Smith. They had a son, named Seth, who also played with Chris. Then there was Dora Tillson, who had two boys. One boy's name was Kevin, and the other boy's name was David. David and his mother did not get along, so David spent a lot of time at our house with our son, Chris.

There came a time when Leona was working for a couple who lived in Pleasant Valley. Their names were Ed and Goldie Shurmberg. Ed did not sleep much at night because he had a lot of pain in his legs, and his wife, Goldie, had heart problems and needed to sleep. So Leona was hired to sit with Ed.

One evening, when Leona went to work, Chris and David were upstairs in Chris's room. I don't remember what they were doing; they may have been playing a game. But when I got ready to go to bed, I was going up the stairs, and David was mouthing off to me. I told him I was going to bust his hind end, and he told me that I could not do that. At that point, I told him that he had said the wrong thing. When I got to the top of the stairs, I went into Chris's room, and Chris was lying in bed. I got David down on the floor and started whipping him. As things continued, I told David, "No one tells me I cannot do anything because if they do, I will do it just to prove them wrong." After whipping David, I went into our bedroom, and as I was lying there, I could hear Chris telling David, "You should have kept your mouth shut," because I think Chris was already aware of what I would do.

Before I went upstairs that night, I had been putting together some advertisers for a friend of mine, but I had not finished them all before going to bed. But when I got up the next morning and went downstairs, the advertisements were completely finished and ready to go. The next time I saw David, he told me that he had become bored and wanted something to do, so he went downstairs and finished the advertisements. I told him thank you and that I appreciated what he had done for me. From that point in time, David would do anything that I asked him to do. At one point, it even went so far that David told me that he wished I had been his father, which made me feel very good.

A short time after we had moved into the apartment, we were asked by the management if we would be willing to move into another apartment because there was someone in a wheelchair who needed the handicapped apartment we had lived in when we first moved there. The manager told us that they were going to have to put indoor-outdoor carpet in the handicapped apartment because of the wheelchair. So they told us if we moved into a different apartment, they would take the carpet out of the apartment we had lived in and put it into the one we were moving into, which they did.

When we moved into the other apartment, we were still living in the back row of all the apartments on the hill. There was a handicapped apartment next to ours. As it turned out, Leona and Chris knew the lady who lived there, but I did not meet her until that point in time. Her name was Susie Nimo. I soon found out that she had been our son, Chris's, Head Start teacher when he was in preschool. As the summer went on, Chris had a lot of fun playing with the friends that he had made while we were living at the apartment. Some were new friends, and some were friends he had known for a long time. As the new school year approached, it would mean a new environment for Chris with new teachers, new classmates, and a new school. Once he started at Unioto, Chris could then ride the bus back and forth to school, and his mother and I no longer had to take him to school.

The first day of school for Chris was probably rather normal. The first evening after school turned out to be rather strange. Once we had finished eating our supper, the three of us were sitting in the kitchen, filling out papers that Chris needed to take back to school the next day. Since the weather was warm, we had our sliding glass door open on our patio, which also had a sliding screen in it, but the screen was closed. But we could get there by the door being open. Since we lived in the back row of the apartments, there was a big field behind them where the grass had been cut because there had been an escaped prisoner from the prison over on State Route 104. I do not remember whether it was CCI or RCI, but one is on one side of 104, and the other one is on the other side. As the three of us were sitting at the table, our neighbor Robin Castle came over to see if she could borrow a plunger. When she walked into the kitchen, she happened to look down at the floor, and then she asked if we had a new pet, and we said no. Then the three of us sitting at the table looked down and saw a snake on the floor underneath the table, and the three of us were barefoot. Chris jumped up on the chair he was sitting on and then ran across the top of the kitchen table, and I moved faster than I'd ever moved before. Leona moved just a little bit faster than I did because we were all afraid of being bitten by the snake. Robin called her husband, Tracy, and he came over. He was able to get it into a jar and put a lid on it. At that point, we did not know whether or not there might be another snake somewhere in the apartment, so we called the game warden, and he came and checked it out. Of course, Chris was afraid and did not want to stay at the apartment that night, so he went home with his grandparents, and his grandfather took him to school the next morning. The house was checked out, and there were no more snakes in there, which we were thankful for.

The next afternoon, after Chris got home from school, the three of us drove on Lick Run Road to the home of Dana and Edna Pritchard, who were Leona's aunt and uncle on her father's side. When we got to their house that afternoon, Leona and I were outside talking to her uncle Dana to see if he knew what kind of snake it was. He told us it was a baby copperhead. He told us that the venom in the baby copperhead was more potent than in a large copperhead because the snake was smaller. Thankfully, we never saw any more snakes after that.

A short time later, a new manager took over at Overbrook Park Apartments. Her name was Josephine Swiggit. One day, when I was down at the office checking the mail because the mailboxes were in the lobby of the office, I got to talking to Jo. That was when I realized that I had heard of her before. Several years before, there was a gentleman who lived at our house, 772, who wanted his yard leveled up. The gentleman's name was Dave. He had asked my dad to haul several dump truck loads of dirt to his house, and then we had to level out the yard with my father's dozer.

When we had finished the job, Dave told my father that he owned a motel close to Nashville and said if we wanted to make a trip to Nashville, he could get us tickets to the Grand Ole Opry. So a short time later, my sister, Tracey, her fiancé, Lawrence Rucker, whom we called Huggy, myself, and my mother and father took that trip to Nashville. We had a good time. The motel where we stayed was in Kingsport, Tennessee. We did a lot of sightseeing when we were in Nashville. One of the places we visited was the original Ernest Tubb record shop. While we were there, I bought myself a cowboy hat. I also saw the stage they used for the Midnight Jamboree. We also took a ride on a paddlewheel boat down the Cumberland River, visited Opryland, and went to Twitty City. It was a nice place to visit with a lot to see. Conway Twitty was not home, and a short time later, he passed away while on tour. We had also talked about going to Memphis to visit Graceland but changed our minds and did not go to Graceland after all.

The manager of Overbrook Park Apartments was replaced by someone new. The new manager's name was Josephine Swiggit. When she first started managing the apartments, I did not realize that there would be a connection to something that had happened in the past. Our mailboxes were in the lobby of the office. We would have to walk down the hill every day to check our mail. One day, the manager happened to be in the office when we were doing so. That was when Leona and I got to meet her for the first time. One day when I was checking the mail and she was in the office, I got to talking about having made the trip to Tennessee and having stayed in the motel in Kingsport. At that point, I had told Jo that we had made the trip to Tennessee when a gentleman named Dave had told my parents that he owned a motel down there and could get us tickets to the Grand Ole Opry. But the other reason we went on the trip was to get the money that Dave owed my father for the work we had done in the front yard of his house. When Dave went to pay my father, he was told that the money he was going to use to pay my father was his mother-in-law's money. As Jo and I were talking, she told me that she had owned that motel when we had made that trip to Tennessee years before. So once again, even though I did not know it, that was another time when things seemed to have come full circle.

Once the new manager took over, I think everyone else who lived there felt like Leona and I were kissing up to her because the complex was getting some new things, and Jo had asked Leona and me if we would like to have a new stove for the kitchen. So we got a new stove. Then they were getting a new set of cabinets, and she asked if we wanted the new set of cabinets as well, and of course, Leona said yes. So that is why everybody thought we were kissing up to the manager, which was really not the case, but they did not know that.

There came a time when we must have had a mouse or a rat in the apartment. We had a storage place where we kept our deep freeze, and we had other stuff in there besides that. The ladies' group of Pleasant Valley Plug Run Church had published a cookbook. The sales of the cookbook were just one of several ways that they were trying to raise money to build an addition to the church. One of the other ways that they were trying to raise money was by selling candy bars. At that point in time, the church did not have inside plumbing. Ron Posey and I were two of the people who sold the most candy bars. I would probably, on average, sell about one case a week. Of course, I ate some of them too, but I paid for them just the same. There were no freebies. But as I mentioned previously, we had a storage area in the apartment where we kept our deep freezer. We had put a pumpkin in there, and there was one of the church's cookbooks lying in the freezer.

One day, when we looked in there, something had been eating off of the pumpkin, and someone or something had also been eating the cover of the cookbook. Even though we were not supposed to have a cat, we got one anyway, and the cat's name was Thomas. One day, Kenny Johnson, the maintenance man, came up to check something at the apartment and asked us if we had a cat. We told him we did have a cat, but Kenny told us he would not tell, and he did not tell.

At the end of October in the fall of 1992, Leona, Chris, and I decided to take a trip to Sciotoville, which is where Leona's aunt and uncle, Paul and June Truman, lived. We went down on a Friday night and stayed until Sunday. When we got up Sunday morning, Paul built a fire because it was cold that morning. Then Leona and I went to church with Paul and June. We stayed for dinner. By then, it was getting colder, so we had to head home because we knew our apartment would be cold. But little did we know what was ahead of us weather-wise that winter.

When we got home that day, our apartment was cold, and we had to turn the furnace on as soon as we walked in. The weather was so bad and so cold that we did not turn our furnace off until either the last of March or the first part of April in 1993.

When we got home on Sunday night, that was October Thirtieth. The next day was the Thirty-First, and we had snow the next day. The weather that winter was very bad because we had our first snow on the Thirty-First of October 1992.

That winter ended up being very bad, and we had a lot of snow. They did not clean the snow out of the parking lot, so we did not walk down the hill to check the mail. The only thing that Leona and I could do was just sit in our kitchen, listen to the radio, work on jigsaw puzzles, and hope the electricity did not go off. One day, when the schools were closed because of bad weather, a photographer from the *Chillicothe Gazette* stopped by the apartment complex. Chris and some of his friends were playing in the snow, and Chris was sliding down the hill in the snow, and his picture was in the newspaper. The winter of 1992–1993 was so bad, it reminded me of the blizzard of 1978–1979 because we were stuck inside for so much of the time. The three of us were glad when winter finally ended and spring came.

The time finally came for our interview at the Ross County Welfare Department. When we went in for our interview, we were sitting and waiting to be called back. We happened to notice something on the bulletin board. It was a flyer talking about doing daycare in your home for other people who had children and the parents had no one to watch the children while they worked. So Leona and I took down the number, and we called to get information about the program. We decided we wanted to try it, so we applied and were approved to do daycare in our home.

There was one little boy whom we watched for a couple of months. His name was Cameron, and his mother's name was Mia, but he was the only child we watched while we were doing the program. The only bad thing about living in the apartments was that the walls were so thin that you could hear everything that was going on. If the neighbors were fighting, the other thing was almost every night, you could hear people throwing beer bottles in the dumpster because a lot of the people drank, but they were good people just the same. A little later, we got new neighbors who moved in next door. Their names were Ernie and Shannon.

After Leona and I had gotten married and moved into the apartments at Overbrook Park, her parents decided to move as well. They purchased a brand-new mobile home and moved it to Kenowa Village, which is located in Pleasant Valley behind the Cavalier skating rink. There was a time when Leona and I were talking, and it was when President Clinton was running for his second term as president of the United States, and he had been talking about having people on welfare work for food stamps. As we were talking, I told Leona that if the only thing we were going to get was food stamps if she had to go to work to get them, then she might as well get a job and make some money.

One day, when we went to her parents' house to visit, I stayed in the car while she went in to talk to them. When she told her mother she was thinking about going to work, her mother told her she didn't need to go to work, that she already had money and she didn't need to go to work.

When Leona came back to the car, she was very upset by what her mother had said to her. Heading back home, I told her that was our decision and not her mother's decision to make. I do not remember how Leona found out, but one day, as we were driving out Western Avenue, we looked at this sign, and it said they were taking applications for a Salvation Army Thrift Store that was opening in a building that had formerly been a car dealership. So we looked at the dates they were taking applications, and we decided that Leona could go down and apply to see if she could get a job. It was the first regular job she ever had, but when she came back from the interview, she told me that she had gotten the job and was going to have to work every day to get the building ready for the opening of the thrift store.

Little did we know that that would change both of our lives for the better. When Leona just started working, of course, they cut our food stamps, but that was okay because we thought she was going to have to work for them anyway. When she started working, she was making $4.50 an hour. When Leona started, it was in March of 1995, but it took them about a month and a half to get ready for the grand opening of the store because they had to price all the merchandise that they were going to sell and hang the clothing on hangers and put them on rolling racks so that customers could walk through the store and make the selections they wanted.

There were several other things that were good for Leona as well. One was that she made a lot of new friends. Leona's two best friends were the two bosses that she had, and both of them happened to be named Mary. One was Mary Spencer, who had gone to the same school as Leona, but I do not know whether they were friends at that time or not. The other Mary was Mary Copas. I don't remember what year it was. We were still living in Overbrook Park Apartments, and it happened to be on her anniversary. Leona had worked that day, so I was waiting for her to get off so we could celebrate, and I was at home with her son, Chris. As the evening grew later, he kept asking where his mother was, and I said I did not know. At that time, she was carrying a cell phone, so I called, and she answered the phone. I asked her where she was, and she said Mary Copas had tickets to a concert, and she had gone with Mary to see Ricky Skaggs in concert in Columbus, Ohio, to which I said, "Leona, did you forget that this is our anniversary?"

Of course, that brings up a memory of our first anniversary. Leona had gone on a diet and lost weight because she was going to have to have her gallbladder removed, but she had ulcers, so she had to get them healed up before they could do the gallbladder surgery. The day that she had the surgery was April 10, which also happened to be her parents' wedding anniversary. So we were all sitting in same-day surgery waiting for her surgery to be over. Since our first anniversary had been in March of 1992, and we did not do anything to celebrate, when we finally did celebrate, her parents, Leona, and I all went out to dinner at a Mexican restaurant. So the night that she and Mary Copas went to the concert was another anniversary where things turned out differently than expected.

It was probably about six months later when one afternoon, Leona and I had gone over to visit Dora Tillson, the mother of Chris's friend David. As we were sitting and talking, I became very ill and said we needed to go home. When we got back to our house, I went into the bathroom and started throwing up green vomit. After coming out of the bathroom, I sat down and told Leona that she was going to have to take me to the emergency room.

When we got to the hospital, I was sitting in the waiting room when all at once, I knew I was going to get sick again. So I told them to give me something to throw up in. Of course, they did as I asked, but then they took me straight back into an examination area. At that point, they told me that I was having a gallbladder attack. Leona had hers taken out before, and now it was my turn. As luck would have it, I had the same doctor that Leona had, and I also ended up being in the same room she had been in. Unfortunately for me, I have had a lot more problems since I had my gallbladder removed than Leona did.

There came a time when we were still living in the Overbrook Park Apartments when Leona began to have other health problems. So we had to make an appointment with another doctor, Joy Shields, at Berger Hospital in Circleville. When we went to see her, we told her that Leona was having problems with bleeding, and at first, she didn't want to do anything about it. But Leona and I both kept insisting that we wanted something done. Finally, Dr. Shields relented and agreed to perform a hysterectomy. I think Leona and I thank God every day that we insisted that Dr. Shields perform the surgery because if she had not done so, Leona might not be here today. And because the surgery was performed at Berger Hospital, I stayed with Leona until she was released from the hospital. As things worked out, it was a good thing I was there because when Dr. Shields came into the room a couple of hours after surgery, she informed me that they had given Leona too much medication to put her to sleep. She told me to keep an eye on her, which I did, but when she woke up, she was so groggy that she could not feed herself. So I had to do it.

Two days after surgery, Leona was allowed to go home but was told that she could not go up and down stairs. So that meant we had to move the bed downstairs into the living room, and I slept on the floor beside the bed to make sure she was alright. It was about two or three weeks after the surgery that we got a call that Dr. Shields wanted to see us because the office had called but would not say why.

Dr. Shields wanted to see Leona, so we drove to Circleville to find out what she wanted.

When she walked into the room, she was crying and said that when they had done the hysterectomy, they had found two spots on the underside of her uterus: one was the size of a dime and the other the size of a quarter. Dr. Shields then told us that the two spots were cancerous. So as I said earlier, Leona and I thank God every day that the surgery was performed because if not, the cancer may have never been found. Once again, that was another time when God was with Leona and me both, and he was watching out for us. So please remember that God is aware of everything that is going on with each and every one of us.

In 1995, Leona and I decided to try to get our son, Chris, his own car because he had started dating. So if he wanted to go to his girlfriend's house, we would have to take him there and either wait for him or go back and pick him up. Ernie and Shannon, our next-door neighbors, had gotten another car and had decided to sell the one they had previously had. So Leona and I talked to Ernie to find out how much he wanted for the other car for our son, Chris. We made a deal and ended up buying the car, but the car was still sitting in the parking space that originally went to Ernie's apartment. Each apartment was allowed two parking spaces. Once we had purchased the automobile, and it legally belonged to us, there must have been someone who was mad at Ernie because one night after dark, we realized that the tires had been slashed on the car. At that point, we had to call the Sheriff's Department, and a deputy came out to talk to us. So Leona and I were standing on the sidewalk talking to the deputy. We told him we thought we knew who did it, and he said, "If you didn't see him do it, then you can't prove it."

At that point, I said, "Then there is nothing we can do," and he said no.

Then I asked him, "Then the only alternative I have is to move?" and he said yes. So even though we liked the apartment, we decided to move because we didn't know whether our things would be safe or not.

There were a couple of other things that happened while we were still living at Overbrook Park Apartments. One night, we were running late for church, and as we got to the Y on Anderson Station Road and Route 50, there had been an accident in that very spot. If we had been on time, we could have possibly been in the accident, but it was another time when God was taking care of us.

One Wednesday evening, when Leona and I were headed to church, as we were driving out the highway, a group of deer came out of the field and ran across the road in front of us. There were eight altogether; we missed seven of them, but the eighth hit the side of our car and put a dent in the door. The car was not badly damaged, so we went on to church that night. When we left church and headed home, either the deer had not been injured and run away, or someone had stopped to pick it up.

There was another occasion when the church was having a baptism in a creek off Route 50. After it was over, Leona and I were returning home, and the traffic was down to one lane because of road repair. We were stopped, waiting our turn to get into the other lane to proceed towards home, when a car rear-ended us as we were sitting still, waiting our turn. The car that rear-ended us was a Norris dealership car, and the driver got out. As he was talking to Leona, our pastor, Reverend Mosley, came up to see what was going on. The gentleman offered her $50 not to say anything and said he would fix her car, but Reverend Mosley told her not to do it, which was the right thing.

The next day, the gentleman called and said he was not going to fix our car, so I went down and filed a claim in small claims court against him. When the Norris dealership found out about it, they called us and said that they would fix our car, which they did. And I later found out that the salesman had lost his job. But as I said earlier, we were in the process of moving.

Chapter 12

As Christmas approached in 1995, my grandmother told me that she wanted to take me shopping for my Christmas present. So she stopped at the apartment one day and picked me up. As we were shopping, she told me that she had something to tell me, and she wanted me to hear it from her and not from somebody else. She then told me that, once again, she had cancer. That year, she bought me a black suede vest and a pair of black suede gloves. While we were still in the store, she told me she was going to start taking treatments for lung cancer. There was one thing she wanted: she wanted a permanent in her hair because she was afraid she might lose her hair while taking the treatments. And I told her if that was what she wanted, I would talk to Leona.

As we were getting ready to leave the store, she remembered that she had put her purse down somewhere. It was a good thing we remembered because there was two hundred dollars in it, which was all the money she had. When my grandmother dropped me off, I went in the house and told Leona what my grandmother had told me about the cancer and wanting the permanent in her hair before she started her treatments, and that was the only time I ever told Leona that she could not say no. My grandmother was having trouble eating, but I told her that if she would bring the medicine that they gave her to help her eat, I would fix dinner for her, and she told me if I fixed it, she would eat it. On the day that Leona put the permanent in her hair, I made meatloaf, mashed potatoes, corn, and lima beans, and she ate it.

Sometime later, my sister Tracey called and asked me if I would come out and have dinner with her and my grandmother. If Tracey fixed the dinner, I told Tracey that I would. So she picked me up early one afternoon, and we drove out to my grandmother's. Leona told me that she would come out later and pick me up.

Tracey fixed pork chops, mashed potatoes, and vegetables. Tracey and I were sitting at the kitchen table eating, and my grandmother was sitting in the living room where she was eating. All at once, my grandmother started throwing up. My sister had to clean up the mess, and when she came back to the table, she looked at me and said, "What did I do wrong?"

I told her that she had not done anything wrong, and it was not her fault; it was just that our grandmother could not keep anything down. Later that evening, Leona came to pick me up, and my sister had left shortly before that. I told my grandmother that before we left, we were going to have prayer with her. As we were getting ready to leave, I went on my knees in front of the chair, and my grandmother, Leona, and I prayed. I told the Lord to take care of my grandmother. As I did that, I knew that He would do so however He saw fit.

But there is one thing that Leona and I have never forgotten, even after all these years, and that was that my grandmother looked at Leona and said, "Please take care of him for me," to which Leona replied, "I will," and she always has. I think Leona and I both realized that my grandmother did not have a lot of time left, and I think she realized that by what she had said to Leona. The other thing that I remember about that night was that Leona cried on the way back home.

Christmas in 1995 was to be the last Christmas before my grandmother passed away in 1996. Leona and I were still living at Overbrook Park Apartments. My grandmother's health began to deteriorate to the point that she could no longer live by herself. So at that point, she went to live with my mother and father in the house they had built after selling Huntington Grocery.

By that time, she had started taking the treatments for lung cancer, and the treatments began to burn up her throat. At that point, it became harder for her to eat because she could not swallow anything. I remember one day when I was at home and called her to check on her. When she got on the phone, I asked her what she was doing, and she said, "I have been sitting at the kitchen table for two hours trying to eat a piece of pie." At that point, I began to realize that if she could not eat, that was a very bad thing because she had always been an old-fashioned cook who cooked everything from scratch, and the one thing she loved to do was eat. At that point, I decided to put a second telephone line in the apartment with a separate number, which I was really not supposed to do, but under the circumstances, I wanted to be able to talk to her anytime I wanted to, or I wanted her to be able to talk to me anytime she wanted to. So that way, there was always an open phone line. As time went on, Leona and I began to go out to my mother's at least one day a week to visit my grandmother, but before we would leave the house, I would call her and ask her what she wanted. A lot of the time, she would say she wanted a milkshake and a hot dog from the Dairy Queen. And if that's what she wanted, that's what she got. A lot of the time, she would only eat one or two bites of the hot dog, but that did not matter; she still got whatever she wanted.

There was one afternoon when Leona had to go to the emergency room at the hospital, and it just so happened that my grandmother was also in the hospital because she had gotten a hot dog stuck in her throat, and they had to remove it. Once I realized that Leona was going to be in the emergency room for a while, I told her I was going upstairs to check on my grandmother. Down the hallway, my mother happened to hear me coming, and she stepped out into the hallway and said, "I have never been so glad to see someone in my life." At that point, my mother was giving her fits because she wanted to go home, but they had not yet removed the hot dog from her throat. At that point, my mother said she was going downstairs to be with Leona in the emergency room. I was sitting on the chair at the foot of her bed.

By this point in time in the story, Leona and I had left Pleasant Valley Plug Run Church for several different reasons. One was because Reverend Mosley's wife, Dorothy, got up in front of the church one day when the church was raising money for the expansion, and she said that the congregation was not doing enough to help out, and it was all up to Reverend Mosley. This made me feel that what I was doing and what Ronnie Posey was doing by selling candy bars did not matter to her, and I felt like I was being thrown under the bus. There had been a time when Chris was playing baseball for Post 62 because the doctor at Children's Hospital told us to find something that our son, Chris, wanted to do to burn off the excess energy he had because of the medicine he was on for his attention deficit disorder. And if they had rainouts, the games had to be made up on Sundays, and if Leona could not be with Chris at the game, I had to be. At one point, Reverend Mosley and I had a long discussion about it. As Leona and I left church after service one Sunday night, we felt like it was time to leave and go somewhere else, which we did. But we did not ask for our membership to be removed.

We then started attending Reverend Stanley Kennedy's church on Monroe Avenue. There I was one night, thinking about what my grandmother was going through with the fact that she could barely eat. I stood up and asked the church to pray that the Lord would take her home because I felt it was unfair to keep her here with the way she was suffering. And that was one of the hardest things I ever had to do in my life, but I felt that if I was the Christian I claimed to be, then it was unfair of me to keep her here because I felt I was being selfish, and that was not what God would have wanted. As I had said a few lines back, at one point, I was sitting at the foot of her bed in the hospital, and she told me she wanted to go to the bathroom but to watch because she was not supposed to get out of bed. In the bathroom, I realized she had on a pair of stockings, something like pantyhose, but she did not have them pulled all the way up. So when she got to where I could, I reached over and helped her pull them up, and then she went around the bed to sit in a chair. After sitting there for a few minutes, she told me she was cold, so I got a blanket and covered her up. At this point, she told me I was going to get into trouble, and I told her that I would not get in trouble for helping her. At that point, we began to talk, and she told me she knew she was going to die. She said, "I don't want to die, but I know I'm going to, but I want to go home to die."

But I told her, "You cannot live by yourself." She would not have been able to do so because she was so frail and so weak.

A little while later, she decided to get into the bed and lay down. She had an IV in, and she had it stretched across the bed like half an X, and I was afraid she was going to pull it out of her vein. So I got up and tried to fix it, and again she started to tell me I was going to get into trouble. So I fixed the IV hose, and again I told her they were not going to do anything to me for helping her.

Since it was getting late, I knew I was going to have to go back downstairs and check on Leona. As I was getting ready to leave, she told me she was in pain, and I told her I would tell the nurse to get her something for the pain. Little did I know then that that would be the last time I would see her alive, except for the night just before she passed away. And at that point, I'm not sure exactly how much she was aware of. The night I saw her in the hospital was on a Wednesday night. When I went back downstairs to the emergency room to check on Leona, my mother was still there but said she was going home and she was not going back upstairs to check on my grandmother.

That following Tuesday afternoon, I was at home when my mother called and said that if I wanted to see her, I had to come at that point. So I called Unioto School and told them to tell him to come home since we needed the car, and he had taken his mother to work that day and driven the car to school. When he got home, I told him what was going on, and that we needed to go up to the Salvation Army thrift store and pick up his mother. I had called the Salvation Army thrift store before Chris got home with the car and told them what was going on, but I told them not to tell Leona, that I would tell her after I got there. When I did get there, I totally didn't know what was happening, and we needed to go to my mother's as quickly as possible. So we headed back out Route 50 and across Blain Highway, doing about eighty miles an hour.

When we got there, I went into my grandmother's room, and her sister Nina Jean, Sam, and Little Helen were there. My mother had to give her pain medication to keep her comfortable. At the same time, she was trying to call the doctor, but she could not get ahold of him. Reverend Mosley showed up, and he was there as well. Leon and Chris stayed until approximately ten in the evening, and then they left to go home because Chris had school the next day.

My mother had told my uncle Wayne, who lived in Florida, and told him what was going on, and he was on his way up from Florida with his two boys, Dale and Marcus. They got there about midnight. Wayne and his two boys walked into the room where I was sitting at the foot of the bed, and Wayne said to her, "Mom, if you can hear me, squeeze my hand." And she did. And then he said, "Dale and Marcus are here, we're all here."

At that point, she took about two breaths and was gone. Before they had gotten there, she had what they call death rattles when she was breathing, but once she knew they were there, her passing was one of the most beautiful things I had ever seen. My mother told me later that she wished she had taken a picture of her lying in the bed because she did not look like she was dead; she just looked like she had gone to sleep.

At that point, I left the room and went to the living room and stretched out, and I was carrying my cell phone. So I called Leona, and when she answered the phone, I told her that grandmother was gone. My mother had to call the undertaker to come and get my grandmother's body and take it to the funeral home, but once they did, everything settled down, and everyone finally went to bed. Leona then came to pick me up, and I went back home. One thing that happened during the time of my grandmother's funeral: Mary Copas, Leona's boss at the Salvation Army, came to the funeral home the night of my grandmother's viewing, and she gave Leona three days off to be with me because she knew I would need her. Along with that, she gave me twenty dollars and told me it was so I could buy something to eat, and that was something that she did not have to do, but I am thankful that she did.

My grandmother passed away on May 14, 1996, a week before my forty-third birthday. For the next couple of years, I did not look forward to my birthday because it was the week after my grandmother had passed away. As time has passed, it is less painful to think about, but it is something that I will never forget.

As things began to return to normal and Leona returned to work, Leona and I put in an application at Tiffin Estate, which was another apartment complex next to Overbrook Park, and that was where we moved. We also originally lived in a handicapped apartment there. One day, a friend of ours named Debbie Estep came to visit, and she did not know that Leona was working. But once again, God's timing was perfect. Kristy Rardin, a friend of ours, had told Leona that Frontier Community Service was hiring. While Debbie was at the apartment, Leona had called, and she was crying. She told me that they had taken her off at the register and put her back in the back again, hanging and tagging clothes, and they had not given her a reason for doing this. When I hung up the phone, I asked Debbie if she would take me out to Frontier to pick up an application, which she did. The office happened to be downstairs, so I got someone from the office to give me an application to fill out. We then drove back to our apartment and filled out the application. I then asked Debbie to take me up to the Salvation Army thrift store and have Leona sign the application so I could take it back to Frontier.

When I took the application back to turn it in, they pulled the boss out of a meeting, and he talked to me in the stairway. I explained to him that Leona had taken care of several other people before and I also told him that I felt that she had good people skills. I also told him that she was working at the Salvation Army Thrift Store but that she was hoping to find a better job.

As I had mentioned earlier, we bought a car for our son, but Leona and I bought another car as well. About two weeks after filling out the application for the job at Frontier Community Service, Leona found out she got the job at Frontier Community Service. Leona was making four dollars and fifty cents an hour when she gave her two-week notice at the Salvation Army Thrift Store. She started out making four dollars and twenty-five cents an hour at the Salvation Army Thrift Store, so she only got a twenty-five-cent raise in almost five years there.

I am thankful to have the grandmother I had because I lived with her most of my life. As I said earlier, from the time I was seventeen years old, my mother had told me that if I wanted to live with my grandmother, I could do so, and we had a lot of wonderful memories and enjoyed a lot of good times together. So that was another time when God put a person in my life whom I needed.

When each and every one of us can look back, we can probably find people throughout each of our lives who were very important in many different ways.

Leona was still working at the Salvation Army thrift store, and a couple of years before, I was working as a bell ringer at Christmastime for the Salvation Army on Fourth Street in Chillicothe, Ohio.

Living in Tiffin Estates was nice. Leona and I met several people who became friends. There were two people who were in wheelchairs; their names were Micky and Angela. We had two other friends; their names were Ray and Bee. Leona and I started out living in a handicapped apartment, as we had done at Overbrook Park, but once again, we were asked to move into a regular apartment, which we did, so Ray and Bee could have the handicapped apartment. Again, we were living in a regular apartment.

There was a time when Leona's mother and father decided to sell their trailer, and I do not exactly know why. I think it was because it was getting harder for her dad to take care of it. At that point, they also moved into Tiffin Estates. The apartment they moved into was kind of up the hill on the other side of the parking lot. They did not live there very long, but while they were living there, Leona's father had a heart attack and was taken to the hospital. I can still remember that night because once we saw the emergency squad at the apartment, Leona, Chris, and I took an ambulance to the hospital.

While our father was in the emergency room, he died, and they had to resuscitate him. A day or two later, they had to put in a pacemaker and a defibrillator. That was the second bad thing that happened to him. The first one was when we happened to be on a family picnic at Tar Hollow, and most of the family members were there. However, Leona, Chris, and I had already left to head home that afternoon. When we got home, we got a phone call letting us know that Leona's father had fallen off the back of a pickup truck and was taken to the emergency room with a broken collarbone. At that time, I used to tease Leona's father that he was trying to act like a teenager. That afternoon, we knew we shouldn't have.

After Leona's father had his heart attack, her parents decided to move once again. At that point, they moved into a house on Adams

Avenue. There were a couple of other things that happened to Leona and me while we were living at Tiffin Estates. One day, Leona was out walking with one of our neighbors named Pat when she accidentally twisted her ankle so badly that she missed several days of work. Our neighbors Angela and Micky had a nurse dad who came to check on Leona's ankle several times to make sure it wasn't broken and to make sure the swelling was going down before she was able to go back to work.

I remember one of the guys named Todd at the Salvation Army thrift store was trying to date Leona, and she told him she was married, but he looked at her and said that didn't make any difference. Of course, nothing happened, but later, I understood why he wanted to be with somebody else.

I think it was the third year that I had been working kettles for the Salvation Army at Christmastime. Major Betty Sharp was still the officer at the Chillicothe Corps of the Salvation Army. The last day of Christmas Kettles was on Christmas Eve. When I got off, Leona and I had to finish our Christmas shopping. There was a game Chris wanted, so we got the game. Then we went to Sears. When we walked in, they were saying Sears was closing in ten minutes, so we were going as fast as we could. So when we left Sears, the only store that was open was Kmart. It was midnight when we left Kmart, and we were sitting in the Kmart parking lot, wrapping Christmas gifts before going home.

Chapter 13

Even though Tiffin Estates had very nice apartments, it was a situation similar to the one at Overbrook Park apartments in the fact that when we moved in there, we lived in a handicapped apartment, but a short time later were asked to move into a regular apartment because someone else needed the handicapped apartment, and that was the same thing that had happened at Overbrook Park. Although at Tiffin Estates, we were able to have our own washer and dryer, which we had not had at Overbrook Park, so it made it easier to do laundry and was less expensive than going to the Laundromat.

We made several new friends while living at Tiffin Estates. Two of our friends were Micky and Angela, who were two young people who were both in wheelchairs because of a disability. They lived in another handicapped apartment just up from ours, and then there was also Ray and Bea, who were an older couple who needed the handicapped apartment that Leona and I lived in when we first moved there. So once again, we were asked to move into a regular apartment, which we agreed to do.

At one point, Leona's mother and father also moved into a handicapped apartment at Tiffin Estates. When Leona and I first got married, her parents decided to move out of the house they had been living in and bought a mobile home that they placed in a mobile home park in Pleasant Valley. But at some point, they decided to sell the mobile home, I think because it was hard for her father to take care of it, and that was when they moved into the apartment at Tiffin Estates. Their apartment was just up the hill on the other side from our apartment.

One evening, Leona's mother had to call the emergency squad for her father, and he was taken to the hospital. Leona and I, along with our son, Chris, followed the ambulance to the hospital.

When we arrived at the hospital, Leona's father had had a heart attack, had died, and was resuscitated. A day or two later, a pacemaker and defibrillator were placed in him to regulate his heartbeat. A short time later, once again, Leona's mother and father decided to move to a house on Adams Avenue.

A couple of things happened while we were still living at Tiffin Estates. There was a situation in which a water pipe burst in the wall between our apartment and the one next to us. Water was seeping into our apartment and ruining the carpeting, but thankfully, at that point, we had renters' insurance that would have covered any damage to any of our furniture or appliances. But the management of the apartment complex had the carpet in our apartment cleaned and shampooed so that you would have never known that anything had ever happened. There was another handicapped apartment next to the one we were living in, and it just so happened that the people who moved in there, whose names were Pat and Arnold, had been the managers of the mobile home park in Pleasant Valley where the mobile home of Leona's parents had been parked.

One evening, Leona and Pat were out taking a walk when Leona accidentally sprained her ankle, and she was unable to work for about a week. Of course, she was still working at the Salvation Army, even though she had already found out that she was going to get a position at Frontier Community Service. One of Leona's coworkers, whose name was Todd, worked as a truck driver for the Salvation Army thrift store. At one time, he had tried to date Leona, and she told him that she was a married woman. He said that that didn't make any difference. Of course, to Leona, it did make a difference.

Sometime later, Leona and I decided to move out of the apartment to a little house on Hickory Street. Our landlords' names were Jeff and Sandy. As I mentioned, the house was small, but since it was just Leona and me, there was one bedroom upstairs, a living room, a kitchen, and a bathroom downstairs. There was also a room that was like a back porch where we had a washer and dryer and a deep freeze.

Jeff and Sandy also owned a two-story house that was next to the one we were living in. At one point, Jeff asked Leona and me if we would paint the big house next door because he wanted to rent it, and he told us that if we did, he would take three hundred dollars off of the rent for our house that we were renting from them. So Leona and I decided to do it.

Of course, by then, Leona was working for Frontier Community Service. The new job required her to go to work at 4:30 p.m., and she did not get off till 8:30 or 9:00 a.m. But the fact that she started out at Frontier Community Service making $7.50 an hour was a $3 raise from when she had left the Salvation Army thrift store. But the amazing thing about that was that Leona was the last person who was hired by Frontier before it was necessary for a person to have a high school education or a GED, because Leona did not graduate from high school or did not have a GED. So I hope this shows anyone and everyone that with the help of God and self-perseverance, you can overcome anything and everything in your life. Because, as I said, God has a plan and a purpose for each and every one of us, and with God's help, each of us can overcome any obstacle that is placed before us.

Since Leona was working nights at Frontier, the two of us would work on painting the house next door when she got home in the morning or on the days she was off. Also, since the house was two stories, when we started painting, we started upstairs and worked our way down. We would paint the ceiling and paint the walls, and I was on the board, taping and painting the wooden baseboard around the edge of the floor, and I would paint as high up on the walls as I could reach. I painted the stairway one step at a time, painting as I went, including the spindles and the baseboards along the steps. The hardest part for Leona was painting the wood around the edge of the windows in the house because the windows were so tall. But we finally finished the job and accomplished what we were asked to do. Jeff rented the house, but we did not know our neighbors very well. The two of us have never been people to have bothered our neighbors. We have pretty much stuck to ourselves. A short time later, Jeff came by the house on Hickory Street and told us he wanted to sell it, but that he had another house on High Street that we could move into, which we did because we knew we would have the same landlord, and he had been very easy to deal with.

The house on High Street was also very nice, and it was very close to High Street Church of Christ in Christian Union, which was the church that Leona was attending before we got married. That house had a full basement with a hookup for a washer and dryer, a half bath with a shower, kitchen, dining room, living room, one bedroom, and a full bathroom upstairs that had an old-fashioned claw-foot tub. The house also had a big backyard. It was right on the alley, so we could park our car in the backyard instead of on the street.

While we were living at the house on High Street, arrangements were made for me to take some classes at the vocational school on Crouse Chapel Road. Given what had happened, I decided to study computers since I had never used one. It was something new and different for me. The instructor I had in the class was a very nice lady, and as time went on, I began to learn a lot about how to use a computer. I began taking classes in the fall of that year, but as time went on and time drew closer for Christmas Kettles to start at the Salvation Army, I felt I needed to return and do what I had done for several years before. At that point, I told the teacher of the class that I was going to take five weeks off to do Christmas Kettles for the Salvation Army, whether she liked it or not. So she told me if I wanted to, I could do some extra work to make up for the time I would be gone working for the Salvation Army, and at that point, that was exactly what I did. But little did I know how things were about to change because, once again, God had other plans for me.

As I returned to the Salvation Army that year to do Christmas Kettles, there were new officers running the Chillicothe Corps. They were the Wallaces. There was one day when I had arrived for work, and while waiting to leave to go to my location for the day, it was the day they happened to be giving out the food baskets and Christmas gifts that year. As I was standing against the wall, there were chairs lined on both sides of the hallway. The Salvation Army and the church were full of people waiting to get what they were to receive for Christmas that year. All the chairs were filled, and as I stood there looking at the people, I realized how many people needed help that I was not aware of. After arriving at my location for that day, I was sitting there doing my job when God spoke to me and said, "Now I am showing you what I am calling you to do." At that point, I realized that I was not supposed to be taking computer classes and that God wanted me to do something else. When I finally got the opportunity to talk to Leona about what happened, she told me to do whatever God was leading me to do. I thank God every day that she was willing to trust what I knew God was telling me.

One morning, Captain Wallace was taking the kettle workers out himself, and he began to talk to me about what he called a Summer Kettle program, which would help fund some of the other programs that the Salvation Army ran throughout the rest of the year. I do not think anything like that had ever been tried before, but he told me if I wanted the position, I would have to earn it. He was just not going to give it to me.

By that time, we were living in a mobile home in Massieville that was also owned by Jeff and Sandy because, just as before, they had decided to sell the house on High Street. But there was a period of time that I had to wait for things to work out as God intended because, eventually, I was hired as a full-time employee of the Salvation Army. But while I was waiting on God to move, one night, Leona was talking to her mother on the phone, and her mother said that I was a lazy SOB and did not want to work. She then told Leona that she did not want me in her house. Of course, Leona's mother was not aware that I had heard exactly what her mother had said to her. When Leona got off the phone with her mother, I told her that if that was what her mother wanted, then I would not set foot in her house, and I did not set foot in her house for almost three years. But I told Leona that when it came to family functions, she could go, but not to ask me to go because I would not.

On the fateful day of September 11, 2001, I was at home waiting for Leona to get off work from the night before, and I had been watching television while waiting for her to get home. I had seen the planes hit the towers in New York at the World Trade Center. At that point, I knew that then there would be a day that we would never forget, and may we never forget the sacrifices that were made by those people who were lost while trying to save others. I remember when Leona came home that morning, she told me that one of the clients that she takes care of, whose name was Richard, had come into the kitchen and told her. Richard called Leona "mother" because he told her she reminded him of his mother. Leona and Angie, who worked during the day and also showed up for her shift, were in the staff room when Richard was yelling for them to come to the living room, saying, "They are blowing it up! They are blowing it up!" At this point, Leona and Angie went into the living room to watch what was on television and realized that two planes had flown into the World Trade Center towers.

When Leona got home that morning, she picked me up, and we headed back to town because that was her payday, and we had to pick up her check and go pay bills. On this occasion, they were having a meeting at a location in Yoctangee Park. While Leona went over to wait her turn to get her check, I was sitting in the car listening to the radio. While I was listening, they stated that there were two planes missing besides the two that had hit the towers in New York City. One plane hit the Pentagon in Virginia while the other plane crashed in a field in Pennsylvania. But because of what had happened that morning, they told everyone that they could pick up their checks and then leave. Leona and I spent the rest of that afternoon paying bills and doing the things that we had to get done before she went back to work that night.

Later that afternoon, I got a call from Captain Wallace letting me know that he was going to have a special service at the corps for the people who had been killed in the disaster earlier that day. He told me that if I wanted to attend, he would come out and pick me up. I told him I appreciated that very much. That was one of the most somber services I think I ever attended in all my years as a Christian. One of the other nice things that Captain Wallace did was order shirts for all of the members of the corps, I think as a reminder so that we would never forget what had happened on September 11, 2001.

It was about that time that I was hired as a full-time employee of the Salvation Army, and Leona and I became members of the

Salvation Army Church in Chillicothe. This meant that anything I did as far as the Salvation Army was concerned, I was required to be in my Salvation Army uniform.

A couple of nights later, after September 11, I was at home when I got a phone call from Captain Wallace asking me if I wanted to stand kettles to raise money for disaster relief for the people in New York City. I told Captain Wallace that he was my commanding officer, and if he wanted me to stand kettles, I would do it.

Either the next day or the day after, I began to stand kettles at Walmart in Chillicothe, and I was raising so much money that they had to change my kettle at least twice a day. There was one day when Captain Wallace's son, Richie, came to Walmart to bring me an empty kettle and take the one that I had started using earlier that morning. One afternoon, Captain Wallace picked me up himself to take me home. On the way, he told me that there only one dollars in the kettle that Richie had picked up earlier that day, and I told him that there had been five dollars and other larger bills, and I knew that because I always watched what people put in the kettle. After that incident, I was told not to let Richie have the kettle under any circumstances, and if he showed up, I was to call the office.

One afternoon, Richie showed up at Walmart and wanted the kettle, and I told him no and went directly to the service and called the office as I was told to do. When I called, I talked to Captain Wallace's wife, Jill, and once again, I was told not to let Richie have the kettle. He had told me that his mother had told him to come and get the kettle, but after talking to her, I realized that he was lying because she told me she had not sent him, at which point, I said to him, "You had better get out of here, or I am going to call the cops because your mother did not send you to get the kettle, and your father and I know that you have been taking money out of the kettles." At this point, he left and did not return. I probably was at Walmart for about a month or a month and a half, receiving donations for disaster relief.

A short time later, once again, it was time for Leona and I to move, so we moved from Massieville to a home that became available in the city of Chillicothe.

Leona and I moved to 141 East Fourth St, Chillicothe, Ohio, and lived across from the Salvation Army. One night, around 7:30 p.m., we were sitting in our computer room and started singing; we kept singing until 4:00 a.m. At that time, Leona said she felt like God wanted us to have a gospel song in our front yard. Despite not knowing how to plan one, we knew that was what we were supposed to do. Our first song fest happened on September 11, 2001, one year to the day of the New York attack. Leona and I sponsored the whole thing and gave all proceeds to the Salvation Army. So as you can see, God spoke to Leona the same way He would speak to me. We held the gospel song for two more years afterward. God was leading both of us in whatever we were supposed to do.

About the Author

The book tells how God guided me and my wife, Leona, and how God blessed us throughout our lives.